I CHOOSE MYSELF

DEEPTI VEMPATI

COPYRIGHT

DEDICATION

To my parents,
my brother and sisters,
my dogs and friends—
and all of the amazing people around
the world whose inspiration, good energy,
support and love uplifted my soul and
sustained me through these thirty-one years.

CONTENTS

PREFACE

"A journey based on 'I am not enough'
ends up with the unfulfilled promise,
no matter how well you have lived."
– DEEPAK CHOPRA

I'm an Indian American girl. I live in Chicago.

I love people, traveling, nature, and capturing it all through photography.

I speak three languages, Telugu, Hindi, and English.

I am passionate about humanity, individuality, and spirituality.

I'm the hopeless romantic from *Love Is Blind* who opened her heart for the world to see.

And I want to tell my story before and after that moment at the altar.

Here we are in 2022. At the age of thirty-one, I feel compelled to pause, reflect and invite you into my thoughts. I am writing this autobiography for a purpose.

My goal is to go deeper (pun intended), take you beneath the surface, and show you the journey that led me here today. My experiences tested and transformed me in unexpected ways.

I am not writing this to tell a fairy tale but rather to be vulnerable with you in hopes that it resonates. Even if just one person reads this and thinks to themselves, *Wow, I can relate to that experience or thinking,* then my mission is complete.

There have been many moments in my life when I hated myself and so many more when I loved myself. I want to take you along for that ride.

Writing this book challenged me to understand myself. There were moments when specific experiences brought out emotions that I had suppressed for many years. I never thought I would resurface them with anyone, let alone in this way. I am realizing now that there is power in sharing. Some of you may relate to what I've gone through and can find comfort in knowing that you are not alone. I'm proud of myself for being courageous enough to take you through my mind during the dark times and the happy ones.

It has been highly emotional writing these words, but it's also surprising to see how therapeutic it's been. I've discovered more about myself. Putting this story on paper makes it real, and it's helped me find grace within. I've let go of judging my behavior, and I'm now learning that we are all continually healing and constantly working to unlock new levels of ourselves.

When I started writing, the bad moments of life first came to mind; I guess because those have made the most significant impact. Then, going back at it a second time, I could see the good that left me happier on the other side—the light nestled within the darkness. And in that light is where our power lies. I want to share this story of finding my power with you.

ONE PRECOCIOUS LITTLE INDIAN GIRL

"Growing up is losing some illusions,
in order to acquire others."
— VIRGINIA WOOLF

The rocky hilltops surrounding the western outskirt of Madhya Pradesh is where my journey begins—in this central Indian State. The region is known for its beauty, stunning scenery, and tiger parks. They say sometimes you can hear the tiger roars echoing off the hills at night, strangely reassuring you that beyond car horns, buskers screeching at the top of their lungs, and auto rickshaws spewing fumes twenty-four-seven, nature can exist in tranquility just beyond the city outskirts.

In typical Indian culture, the pregnant mom lived with her parents close to the delivery date because fathers didn't provide the same type of support in the first few months of having a newborn—simply because they didn't understand the nurturing aspect of childbirth. I was two minutes away from being born at 4:20 p.m. that January 30, 1991. My grandmother's help was ideal because my mom already had my older brother, Sunny, and the extra help was welcomed.

Sometimes, the grandparents would even move in temporarily to help. The idea was—well, since my grandma had been through the process of raising a child before, she would have the best insider knowledge and be able to help with this newborn and toddler.

I was already a travel baby at three months old, making my way to the capital city of Hyderabad, Andhra Pradesh (Telangana now). It's here my parents lived with my dad's side of the family and where I spent the next eight years of my life.

Sadly, I didn't get to learn much about the place where I was born. Even my early years in Hyderabad are a blur, which is as expected, I think, given my young age at the time.

I asked my parents to help jog my memory of what I was like as a child. My mom told me I was a little preco- cious, even as a baby. I knew what I wanted. I would lay awake and fuss all night long, but as soon as 5:00 a.m. hit, I would be out like a light. She still jokes to this day that this meant I was supposed to be in America, living in a different time zone.

There was no concept of electric cribs that would swing on their own, but I needed movement to fall asleep—in a car, train or bus was ideal. I wouldn't sleep unless I was in motion. My dad would tie a rope to his leg from his bed to my crib to swing me to sleep. And, as soon as he would fall asleep and stop swinging, it was my cue to start crying. The first six months of my life were tough on them, and what they didn't know was that the years to come would be even more challenging.

My parents were givers, though, and they did everything and anything for my siblings and me. My dad tying a rope to his foot to swing me was just one example of how they lived for us. They always put us first to ensure we were the happiest kids.

My parents lived a very simple life; they were taking it day by day to make ends meet. Dad was the youngest of six kids, so I have a huge family with many cousins. In India, living in a nuclear family was not normal back then. We lived with my grandparents (father's side) and my uncle's family. Looking back, I can't even imagine eleven people living under one roof—we lived downstairs, and they lived upstairs. I was close with my grandparents, who often took care of me. We would frequently travel to see my mom's side of the family, too.

It was also common in India to have help from maids and drivers, even if you were not very wealthy. I did not understand this concept of class systems and servants because I would see people as people. My mom once told me about a time we were having a party at my grandparents' while multiple people were working on their terrace in the heat. We were eating good food and drinking chai, and apparently, I looked up at my mom and said, "What about all the people working hard upstairs, amma? Shouldn't they also get some of this food?"

She said she remembers looking at her little four-year-old daughter and thinking, *Wow, you have a beautiful heart.*

So, I took a tray of food and water to them. My

grandma, we call her "ammama" (which means mom's mom), tells me that those workers stayed connected with our family for years, and they would always ask, "Bebamma elagundi?" *How is my little angel?* My parents and grandparents prided themselves on that moment.

Growing up in Hyderabad wasn't always easy. Times were tough and raising three kids was expensive. My dad was an electrical engineer then, and my mom was a chemistry professor. I know what you're thinking; these sound like great professions that would bring in a lot of money. But it didn't pay that much. They also invested in a few businesses where they lost a chunk of their money.

I vividly remember when my dad struggled even to put gas in his motorcycle. It was common in India for people to have motorcycles and scooters in the big city. It was easier to get around and much cheaper than a car. A car was a luxury that we had but rarely used. I guess gas prices are always causing problems no matter what year you're in.

My grandfather (my dad's dad), "tatagaru" as we called him, was a very successful chairman of the State Electricity Board, which equated to stature and money. But his mindset was always centered around education and perseverance. His kids had to be financially independent, and there would be no handouts. So, even though my parents felt, at times, strained to have enough money, they were not given any financial support and had to continue to work hard to earn a living, which was part of the process. They never let us kids get a sense of this struggle. My siblings and I never lacked anything because there was so much love and happiness in our household.

Growing up in a big family was extremely fun. I always had cousins who were my best friends. I clung to the ones who were my age. It was also somewhat harsh because my whole life, I was compared to them, their beauty, their grades, and their habits. My mom always told me I was an old soul from an early age. So, playing with kids my age was tough. I usually ended up hanging outside, riding bikes, and playing in the mud. This pissed my mom off because I would always come home dirty or with a skinned knee. As she was bandaging me, she would always say to be cautious and take care of myself while doing these adventurous activities, but she never let me stop being a kid. She always knew that I was different and that she could never stop me from doing what I wanted. She allowed me the freedom to be myself.

One day after school, when I was six years old, I was not supposed to go home on the auto (equivalent to a school bus, just more open). Instead, I was supposed to wait for my dad to pick up my brother and me when he was done with tennis practice. I couldn't find my brother in the huge schoolyard, so I decided to walk home. I was convinced I knew the way. In my head, I was thinking, *My auto driver takes me this route every day, and I know what I am doing.* It turns out I didn't. My dad and brother were frantically looking for me, and my mom was panicking.

India is very congested with people, cars, and motorcycles everywhere. My mom was convinced I would get kidnapped or lost to the point where I would never be found again. Not knowing where I was for an extended period was a terrifying moment for my parents. My dad drove up and down the streets around the school, trying to find me. My mom hopped on her scooter, too. I was nowhere to be found. After a couple of hours, they drove back down a road they had already driven numerous times, and this time, there I was, walking on the median with traffic all around, going in the opposite direction of home. My dad was equally relieved as he was terrified and angry. My mom later yelled at me, too. This was only the start of the worry I gave them in my thirty-one years.

I wouldn't say I liked going to school. My brother, on the other hand, loved it. Again, this was another reason I made my parents' lives difficult, and my siblings continued to be easy kids to raise. My brother was always brilliant. I, on the other hand, had a different kind of intelligence. I was emotionally mature but hated reading and writing in a structured format. I hated being told what to do, and my rebellious nature was already coming to fruition. We went to an English school, but my first language was Telegu—which we spoke at home. We learned to read and write in Hindi as a school subject. I hated going to class, being around strict teachers, and then coming home to another strict teacher—my mother. She had to literally sit me down and force me to do my homework. I disliked her for it but appreciated her taking so much time to ensure I had a bright future.

My parents were juggling a lot at this time. My little sister, Divya, was only one. Raising three little kids while both parents were working was not common. Typically, women took care of the household. Most of my aunts were this way, but my mom was different. She wanted to do it all.

After a couple of years of a tough life, my mom started

to get uncomfortable with how her life was going. My dad's work led him to Japan, and she was stuck back in India with three kids to raise. I always helped her with taking care of my little sister. I think I did a good job as her babysitter for the most part—although I did drop her on her head once because I thought I could carry her a longer distance than I could. She was heavier than I thought. I guess I overestimated my strength. To this day, we have a running joke where she tells people her head is shaped differently because of me.

I also helped my mom in the kitchen. I loved to cook, and I was happy to be there working beside her. As the days went on, she started planting a seed in my dad's head about moving—not just to another State, but to the other side of the world. To my mom, moving to a new country meant a fresh start. My dad was not keen on this idea. He didn't want to leave his family, friends, and support. My mom didn't either. Yet as the days went on, she was getting unhappier with her living situation and the hardships she was facing. She loved our family and friends, and of course, she would miss all the support. But she felt we could have a better life for ourselves if we moved.

In her research, mom started noticing new job opportunities in the technology field in America, which led her to a major mindset shift. While my dad was in Japan, she started taking computer science classes. When he returned, she forced my dad to take the same classes and change his career path so we could all have a better life. Even though he hated the idea of moving because he had just gotten back permanently from Japan, he started taking computer science classes to become a software engineer. This would lead to more money. And that's how he landed a job in the United States. My mom wanted to wait before looking for a job because she wanted to provide support for us kids and be sure we would smoothly transition into a new environment. Our family was about to take the biggest leap of faith ever.

WELCOME TO AMERICA

"With every broken bone, I swear I lived."
– ONEREPUBLIC

When I first heard my parents talk about America, it seemed so foreign that it may as well have been Mars. This faraway place where we would start a new life meant leaving behind everything that I knew.

My dad was the first to go to America to get the lay of the land. He was there for six months to settle into his new office and find an apartment for us. I was just getting comfortable at my school in India and enjoying my friends, dancing, tennis, and family. And all of that was about to change. It felt like I was losing everything that I had grown to love in my hometown of Hyderabad. But even with these fears, I was still hopeful. I think at eight, I didn't realize what I was about to gain: a new place to explore, new habits to create, and new types of people to meet.

When it was finally time to leave our familiar place behind, I realized the most profound impact came on my parents. They would leave their families, friends, lifestyle, home, and comfort behind so my brother, sister, and I could have a better life. This was what America was about —the land of opportunity.

Arriving in America was an exhilarating moment. We flew from Hyderabad to Frankfurt, Germany, to Chicago, Illinois—a twenty-three-hour journey. My siblings and I were fascinated by planes—what an incredible thing to be getting to do at such an early age. My brother became captivated with the concept of an aircraft, and his curious nature of wanting to learn got him access to the pilot. There weren't that many people on the plane with us, and he started chatting with the flight attendant. She loved my brother and asked him if he wanted to see the pilot. Of course, he was elated. This got him even more excited about this journey. We made the commute a fun one. However, I did witness sadness and a sense of worry in my parents' eyes. They were leaving a lot behind and were unsure of the future. Through this worry, they somehow always stayed positive and powered through.

Our first apartment was a two-bedroom on the fourth floor. With only two bedrooms, we had to share rooms. My brother and I were too old to room together, so he shared a room with my dad, though most nights, my dad slept on the couch. My mom, sister, and I shared the other bedroom.

I still remember my very first day of school in America. Occasionally, when I'm back in my hometown of Bloomington, I visit my old school, which seems small now. But that first day, at the age of eight, the building felt so vast. I might have been a foreigner, but I wasn't foreign to big schools. My brother and I attended one of the most prominent schools in the State back in India—Hyderabad Public School. You had to take a difficult test that qualified you to get in. Thankfully, I didn't have to take this entry qualifying test because there was a sibling clause, and my brother qualified for both of us. (Thanks, Sunny!) But even though I was used to big schools, this was going to be a whole new experience. I was also nervous because my brother was going to be in a different building than me, so I would truly be entering the doors on my own.

Thinking back on it now, I remember feeling scared for the first day but excited—the normal feeling you get when going to a new school. I hadn't yet considered that school life might be very different in this new country.

My mom walked me to Stevenson Elementary school. I wore a colorful checkered blue, yellow, and green dress. My mom put my hair up in pigtails, which she loved doing. Me, not so much. I liked to wear it down, which meant less time getting ready. I was happy that my mom and Divya came to school with me on my first day. I felt more confident knowing they were by my side. I was excited to meet new kids and my new teacher.

When I got there, I soon realized no one looked like me. I was coming into this class mid-year, so the teacher introduced me as a new student and gave me a desk space. One girl that was sitting next to me said hello first. She started saying her name, but I honestly couldn't understand her. Her words were confusing, almost like a foreign language. School was a tough adjustment; I couldn't understand the Americanized English accent.

I was in fourth grade, and I remember being happy to be somewhere new and meeting new people, but I had a hard time understanding my classmates and teacher. This, and the fact that I didn't enjoy school, stressed me a lot. I think that's one of the reasons my mom stayed home with us for that first year in the States, so she could be there for us as we adjusted to this new environment we were thrown into.

Divya was only three years old, so her transition wasn't too hard. Sunny also seemed to be adjusting well to his new school. I was having a tough time. Perhaps it was due to the differences in teaching style from my school in India to here. It is hard to learn something new when you can't interpret what the teacher is saying to you.

On top of all of the normal pressures of school, there was an additional challenge I was facing: I had been put in a classroom with kids a year older than me. This meant the information we were learning was even more advanced, and I was having a hard time understanding most subjects. This made me feel stupid. Inserting myself in the middle of a school year was tough; my classmates had already gotten the chance to get to know each other, and I didn't feel like I belonged. So, my teachers and parents decided I should repeat the fourth grade, this time with my age group.

Retaking fourth grade was a blessing in disguise. This gave me a fighting chance to get to know kids from the start of the grade. It made me feel like I could start fresh, although I felt ashamed. I would see the other kids that went onto fifth grade around the school, and I felt embarrassed. I knew I could have been with them if I had done things differently and paid more attention. Unknowingly, I judged myself realizing only later in life that I needed that situation to happen or else I wouldn't have met certain people and had the experiences I had. The course of my life would have looked so much different.

I had a couple of Indian friends in my new fourth-grade class. This was exciting because those kids better understood what I was going through. My parents became friends with theirs, and we would hang out outside of class. I was getting back to my happy, bubbly self again. I would have fun and try new things. One time I was playing on the monkey bars at the park with my friends and thought I was cool enough to swing on them. Little did I know, my arms could not hold my body weight. As soon as I let go of one hand to swing, I was on the ground a split second later. I broke my arm. Aside from the initial pain, I loved having a cast; it made me feel cool. And to be honest, it was the first time I truly felt alive. Just carelessly living and having fun—I realized that I could overcome pain; I was strong.

The transition into fifth grade was easier. I seemed to be finding my place and enjoying the company of my classmates. I kept the same energy of wanting to learn new things and have fun. I was slightly naughty—though in the most innocent of ways. I started to notice boys. I developed my first crush and would write about him in my diary. We sat in alphabetical patterns based on our last names, and ours were together. I love attending class now, but it was mainly because I could sit close to my crush. Isn't it crazy to think about how one person can make your whole experience better?

I hated physical activity; I was lazy, so physical education was my worst nightmare. I saw running like a pacer as punishment. However, one sport we got to try was roller skating. I was so pumped to try out this sport that seemed much more fun than running. I took my release note home to my parents, begging them to sign it. Anxiously they did.

The next day, I was excited about phys ed for the first time. I was ready to try something new—this was when I realized I loved doing things that filled me with adrenaline. Sadly, I wasn't very good at it. The teacher happened to step away for a moment, and I found myself clinging as hard as I could to the walls of that gymnasium.

A few kids came over to me and said, "C'mon, Deepti, you can do it." These words of encouragement helped me muster the courage to give it a shot. I finally let go of that wall—and fell. This time, I fell on my arm even more harshly and broke it again. I vividly remember being very brave and not crying in front of my classmates. I immediately went to the nurse's office and sat waiting for my dad. As soon as I saw him walking down that hallway, I couldn't hold the tears back. I didn't like to cry, but I knew I was safe with my dad. I remember telling him I was okay and for us to not go to the hospital. The nurse had wrapped my arm for me. I convinced my dad to just go home; I didn't want my injury to be another expense. I remembered last time my parents had to pay a lot for my previous broken arm. I didn't want them to be upset with me again. So, I hid the pain all night. The next day, it worsened, and my dad had to take me to the ER. I later found out that my bone was split, and I had to have surgery to get a metal plate in my arm. My mom was terrified. That scar from the surgery still shows on my left arm today—a constant reminder to me that I can endure pain and that I am strong.

My mom had now started taking classes at Illinois State University because her credentials from India didn't qualify her to be a chemistry teacher here. So, she decided to change career paths with the hope of being able to make more money. She decided to continue pursuing computer science. I often think to myself as an adult how brave my mom was—to travel to a foreign country and go back to school to learn an even more complicated subject, all while being a mother and wife in a completely new environment.

In India, it was common to have a live-in maid—I know that might not be the proper term used today. But there was much more help back in India than here. This help included having assistance with cooking, cleaning, packing lunches, driving to pick up groceries, and getting support from family in times of need. These were the unspoken luxuries that we left behind.

The transition to sixth grade got hard again. The friends I did have at this point moved across town. This may not seem like it was a big deal, but this meant that now my friends were going to a different middle school. Kids from other elementary schools would be combined into one giant middle school. I felt overwhelmed. Not only did I still detest the actual act of studying and being told what to do by teachers, but my mom was also forcing extracurriculars into my life. She said it would improve my chances of finding friends and make my student resume look good. In those moments when she made me join the orchestra and go to tennis lessons, I despised her for it. I was lazy, and she was making me try.

After a couple of weeks, though, I found lots of joy in these activities and looked forward to them. I didn't have to speak; I could just act. I found comfort in making new friends and learning new activities outside the classroom. Kids got to know me in a different way and in a much more relaxing and exciting environment. All of us were there learning something new and getting more practice at an instrument or sport we liked. Physical education was still such a nightmare for me. Not only did it mean having to change in front of the other girls, but it also meant I had to do a physical activity outside of tennis.

When I hit sixth grade, my whitewashing mindset began. According to the Urban Dictionary, "whitewashing is a derogatory term used to describe a minority who has assimilated with western society. The 'whitewashed' person does not necessarily abandon his or her own culture but rather embraces others besides his or her own." I use this term because it was around this time that I remember wanting so badly to be liked by everyone else that I started to adopt a mindset that was more reflective of American values than my family's values.

All I wanted was to fit in, and my body was going through changes that made me feel exceedingly uncomfortable. I was seeing other girls around me blossom much quicker. They were pretty, and I remember my best friend at that time having beautiful boobs. This was when my insecurities started to grow. I would constantly compare myself to all the girls in my classes. I loathed the way I looked and talked. I was a brown-skinned girl with dark hair and brown eyes. My American English was not yet perfect, and I had a bit of an accent. And all of the girls who were popular and beautiful in my eyes were the opposite of me: white-skinned with blonde hair and blue eyes. Day after day, I found myself wishing I looked and sounded whiter.

I still found school challenging, and now I had the added pressure of my parents wanting me to do well enough to get into advanced classes. While my parents wanted me to do well in school, all I wanted to do was to focus on my crushes and making friends to fit in.

My mom got a new job in technology and now became overwhelmed from work, taking care of the household, and my dad, so she didn't have much time to babysit my homework. But even still, that's precisely what she did—sit with me every night after school to study. I knew that if I put in the effort, I would do great things, but my focus was elsewhere. My mom was the reason I got through it. After a long day at work, she would come home, and Sunny would already have his homework done while I procrastinated. My mom and I would sit at the dining room table and read each subject together.

In the seventh grade, I met my best friend at tennis practice; let's call her Kendall. This tennis practice was outside of school. It was a racket club that I joined to master my tennis game. Kendall was the reason why I shifted my language and tone; I learned confidence from her. She was a constant influence in my becoming whitewashed, and her conviction is what I admired most. I wanted to be more like her. She had no rules, no limitations, no boundaries. I loved having her in my life because she would convince my parents to let me go out and do things. I finally started to get a friend group. We even had a name for the group—The Burps. Back then, saying "burp" was somehow cool, I guess. This was a double-edged sword, however.

As the middle school years passed, I got bigger and gained much weight, while everyone else around me seemed to be so much thinner. This was the start of my uphill battle with my body and appearance. I even had a gap between my front two teeth which made me feel embarrassed. I started to notice that my best friend, Kendall, although fun, would put me down constantly with her jokes. I tolerated this because I knew that life would suck without her. She was the outgoing and bubbly type of girl with lots of friends. In comparison, I was the awkward, shy, and quiet one, which was entirely different from my childhood years back home in India.

I started to feel my walls going up and the self-judgment creeping in. Even though I was a little reserved in school, I could show my true personality to my closest friend, Kendall, and my family. I was still gaining the courage to be my authentic self in school. There were certain classmates and teachers that I could be comfortable with, which was enough for me to get through the more challenging classes.

The early years of high school were tough. It made me happy that I had friends who cared about me, and I could start to become myself with them. I was still awkward during some school hours, but I loved the classes where I sat next to my high school crush. I was happy to go to my tennis practices and sleepovers with Kendall. Sometimes, kids in class would bully me because of my weight or how dark I would get during tennis season, but it didn't bother me anymore. I had made good friends that supported me and some who were just as dark as I was.

My parents kept the Indian culture in our household alive. We would do poojas, which meant praying to one of our deities, such as Lord Ganesh. We celebrate Diwali every year, the festival of lights. My name was actually derived from this. "Deepti" means "a bright flame or a person that spreads light to people around them," which was inspired by the light that fills up a room like an oil lamp on Diwali Festival Day. On days when I had friends coming over, I'd ask my mom to change out of her Indian clothes because I was embarrassed. I didn't want anyone to know that my family or I had any uniqueness or that we were different. I didn't realize then that having a rich culture and being diverse was such a beautiful thing. My parents understood the importance of not losing our culture and languages. This is why they would ensure that we frequented back to India almost every other year.

Of all my friends, Derek was my kindest friend. He was compassionate and understood me. I also met him at the racket club playing tennis with a new friend, John. Kendall, Derek, John, and I were great friends. When other kids called me bad names that I didn't even know the meaning of, my friends reassured me not to worry. I got through the social torment and bullying at school with the help of my friends.

One of the challenges that prevented me from spending all my time with my friends was my parents' strict rules. At this time, being at home felt like missing out on exciting opportunities to fit in. All I wanted to do was hang out with Kendall, Derek, and John, but their home rules were different from mine. My parents would give me a 9:00 p.m. curfew while my friends would be out well past eleven or even midnight. Their parents didn't care if their kids were out that late. Mine cared too much, and they tried to protect me and give me structure. "The important thing was to learn and focus on getting better grades," they said. I was angry and frustrated at my lack of independence, and I started to turn to food as a way to cope.

Kendall was the one friend I gravitated toward the most. She was fun, refreshing, and a real "queen bee." But Kendall was also very toxic to me. She would repeatedly comment on my weight and poke fun at the fact that I couldn't run as fast as she could. This highlighted another insecurity of mine. Why were my friends thinner, and I was continuing to gain weight? I didn't understand the concept of weight gain due to my overindulging. My parents tried to prevent me from binge eating, but when they were upstairs in bed, I saw it as an opportunity to raid the fridge and cupboards. Eating became a secret pleasure for me—a way to fill the void I felt whenever I was alone. Food gave me comfort and allowed me to take my focus off my self-loathing and negative inner voice for a while. Food was my escape.

While I was stuck at home at night, my brother would be playing video games or off somewhere with his friends. I found this unfair; his rules differed from mine because I was a girl, and he was a boy. He also had many Indian friends, so my parents trusted their families. They were culturally like us. My mom would say, "Oh, your brother would never do anything wrong."

I was not fond of being treated differently because of

my gender. It was also unfair that I didn't have many Indian kids my age in school. The balance was ultimately uneven. I started to compare my life to my brother's. My resentment toward my parents began to deepen, especially toward my mom. She was the rule maker of the family, and my dad just agreed to what she would say.

I sometimes felt like a caged bird, especially on the weekends. All I wanted to do was go out, be with my friends, and live life; instead, I was stuck at home from 9:00 p.m. onwards. This turned me to food even more. It was the one thing I enjoyed because otherwise, I would sit there and mope about the fact that my friends were calling while out, asking me where I was. Eventually, they stopped calling me during those hours because they knew that there was no chance my parents would allow me to come out. This deeply saddened me, and as a result, I binged more and became even heavier.

While food was my comfort and made me feel good in those moments, the aftermath of it did not. This is when I first turned to bulimia. I can't remember the exact date of this onset, but I remember feeling ashamed that I overindulged and would force myself to throw up all that I had been binge eating. I would do this when my parents were asleep, and no one was around. I was somewhat of a night owl, and I coped with the disappointment of my eating habits by regurgitating. It was the only solution I saw at the time. When the bingeing kicked in, it was as if I had no self-control. My brain would turn off, and my body would take over. I didn't know how to stop this cycle. I never forcedly puked in school or around friends or family. I kept my eating disorder a complete secret for many years—no one knew. Or so I thought.

I wish I had known in those moments that things could have been much different had I decided to focus on the reasons I was overeating instead of getting caught up in bingeing and purging cycles. That's the thing about eating disorders—it's not really about the food. Food is just the mechanism used to cope with bigger internal issues that are not being addressed. Those internal issues filled me with a lot of shame and felt unspeakable. Looking back now, I wish I had had the courage to ask for help.

Progressing through high school made me even more boy crazy; I should blame the hormones. I would try to interact with boys, but no one liked me. At this time, I was so ashamed of my body and what I looked like I would even avoid mirrors. I couldn't wait to get through the days as fast as possible so that I could go home and then to tennis—all my friends would be there. It was the one activity I enjoyed doing—not anything that was school or home oriented.

One night, Kendall had the idea to go to Cedar Point in Ohio. She had a car, and we would get a hotel room and go. There would be boys going with us too. She had a boyfriend, and we had our two other guy friends, Derek and John. We both knew there was no way my parents would allow me to go on an overnight trip unsupervised, let alone with two boys. We had to devise a plan—a convincing one. We took the help of her mom, and she came to my house and lied to my mom. She told her that she would be chaperoning the trip and that I would be in good hands. My mom bought it—I was elated. I am finally getting to do something exciting.

The overnight trip did not go as planned. While driving, Kendall got lost in the cornfields. Back then, we didn't have GPS on our phones, and she was following directions on printed paper from MapQuest. It was a reliable source then, but we weren't doing a good job of following the directions because we were distracted by singing along to the music. Although the journey there was rough, we finally made it. We had the best amusement park experience the next day.

When we returned to our hotel rooms, I got a call from my mom. She said, "I just ran into Derek's mom." She had met her before, during our tennis tournaments. What she said next was extremely clever. She asked me, "Do you have something to tell me?" And my heart sank. I knew I was grounded for life. There was no way I was ever seeing my friends again. I assumed that Derek's mom had told her everything. What we were up to that weekend, who was with me, and more importantly, who wasn't. In reality, his mom hadn't said anything to mine about the trip—apparently, my mother just has an incredible intuition.

I spilled my guts to save face and not get into more trouble for lying. I told her I was so sorry for lying, that no one was watching us, and yes, there were boys here. They weren't even *boys*; they were just my friends. But in her eyes, I had just committed a murder. How dare I sleep in the same room with the boys. These years were tough with my mom because her disciplined nature was a huge hurdle for me. All I wanted to do was rebel and do the opposite of what she said.

I was grounded for six months. And on top of that, my mom no longer trusted Kendall's family. Her mom lied to mine, and that's a big no-no in the adult world. So now, I have lost my freedom and my best friend. I was angry and upset. I became moody and started slacking in my classes. I continued to overindulge in food, and the same cycle escalated. I also began turning to journaling. I always looked inward and had a lot to say but no one to say it to. Where eating was my vice, writing was my liberator and freed me from holding onto my thoughts—and still does today.

CATFISHING

"The life I have lived was no more
than a mask covering the real me.
What has happened was not to
kill me but to reveal me."
– E'yen A. Gardner.

I want to tell you about an experience that fundamentally changed me and how I see myself. This is the most challenging chapter I will ever write. I've never told this story to even one person in its entirety, so to share it with you is a decisive moment for me. These are hard words to write because I feel more vulnerable than I have ever been in my life. But there is immense strength in that. This story may change how you see me, but remember, my actions were that of a sixteen-year-old—almost fifteen years ago. I am a much different person now, and the lessons I learned from the childish behavior I displayed have helped transform me into the person I am today.

There were many moments when I questioned whether I should write this story or not, but I realized that someone out there might relate, and I could impact them to act differently. And that is the real reason why I am choosing to tell it.

I've expressed how much I didn't want to be myself growing up. I always felt like the ugly duckling waiting for the day I could flourish into a beautiful butterfly. I know those are two completely different species, but that's how I felt. I wanted to be anything but in my own skin. I guess I didn't fully comprehend the amount of self-hate I had. I was too young to know I had deep insecurities that stemmed from body image issues. I wanted to be a white, gorgeous, blonde girl. So, that's who I decided to become.

One night on Myspace (which, if you're not familiar, was the first extensive social network to reach a global audience before Facebook, Instagram, and TikTok), I came across this profile of a girl that I thought looked perfect. She had everything going for her. She was stunning, a cheerleader, and seemed like she had numerous friends. She was precisely the type of girl that I wished I was. I am unsure what came over me at that moment, but I wanted to escape my reality so badly that I decided to—virtually— become her. I took her pictures, created a new page, and gave her a new name. I still cannot believe that I did such a thing. The current version of me would never even think to go there, let alone act on it. But that's the beauty of telling this story—showing you that there can be growth and compassion in your mistakes. The significant errors we make impact our lives, force us to be different, and address deep-rooted issues. That's what my story represents.

Let's call her Jessica. If I am being honest, I don't recall what name I gave "myself" as a catfish because I have suppressed these moments of my life completely.

When I first became Jessica, I felt empowered because, in my head, I genuinely thought I was attractive when *I* was being *her*. I loved the idea of being her so much that I started to believe it. I guess you don't realize how influential your mind is and how you have the power to shape your reality. The conversation you have with yourself is the most important one, and my sixteen-year-old self told me that I was now beautiful Jessica.

It still feels wild to me how I was able to become someone else mentally, but that's the thing, I wasn't thinking. I just wanted to crawl out of my skin and put a mask on so that people could see what was inside. I was funny, intelligent, and kind, but no one gave me the chance to show who I was because of my appearance—or so I thought. And, as Jessica, I could show my personality and be myself. Guys would already be interested in Jessica based on her appearance, and then I could add all of my personality behind her. Once they saw how fun I was, they would like me even more.

As Jessica, I started adding boys as friends on Myspace, and they immediately accepted and seemed interested in me. This was tremendously dopamine jolting. Every time I got a compliment, it was like getting a hit of endorphins. I knew the compliments weren't directed at me, but they felt good. I was disassociated with the idea that I was Deepti; I was now Jessica. I showed people my personality but just in a different body.

The first guy I ever started talking to as Jessica, was

extremely attractive, and we were able to have deep conversations. I always knew I was mature for my age and had high emotional intelligence. This is why I craved deep conversations, but unfortunately, before pretending to be Jessica, I had no one to have them with. This was the first guy I could talk freely to, and he understood me and my thoughts. Once I got a dose of how it felt to connect to someone and feel good about a guy, I was addicted. I wanted to talk to others because I felt euphoric and finally got some attention that I would never have as Deepti. That's sixteen-year-old me self-justifying.

I know it's fucked up what I was doing, but the feeling of being wanted and getting attention was too uplifting to give up. I would get messages from guys out of the blue just complimenting my physical appearance; it was an overwhelming dose of serotonin. I honestly just craved friendship more than anything. I wasn't romantic with most of them—just one, which blossomed over some time.

The boy I started to have romantic feelings for, we'll call Tony, was the first guy I talked with outside of Myspace as Jessica. FaceTime was non-existent back then (and thank goodness because, obviously, chatting via video camera wouldn't have been possible without foiling my plans), so we would only talk over the phone. Tony loved my voice and how I spoke so maturely. This excited me because it was *my* voice he was conversing with, not Jessica's. It was *my* thoughts and feelings that he related to. Jessica was just a way to get him to approach me, but my personality and ideas are what kept him interested. My belief that this instance of catfishing wasn't completely wrong because it was my personality that Tony was liking, not Jessica's, is how I justified continuing to be her.

Interestingly, as I embodied Jessica, I was also living my life as me. It made me a better person too. As odd as it sounds, I started gaining the confidence I didn't know I had.

To put it simply, I started living a double life. I would go to school but could not wait to be home so that I could chat with Tony. We built this conversational internet bond, and I could communicate my deepest thoughts with him. I never talked to him about what I was doing or who I was with; I didn't want to integrate Jessica into his mind in that way. I wanted our conversations to be about new ideas and feelings. We talked about how hard life was and his life experiences. He was a rebellious kid growing up, and I was similar. We both felt like we didn't fit into the societal norm, and this was a bonding theme for us.

He told me about his mom and how she was never around or there for him. When he talked about her, I could sense that he wasn't loved the way he needed to be, which negatively impacted his relationships with other people. It made me realize how important my mom was to me. Her toughness was a form of love. It showed that she cared enough to be hard on me even though it hurt her to do so. I started to gain a deep appreciation for all that she did for me. It was easy to take for granted the little things—having someone who makes you breakfast every morning, cleans for you, and does your laundry.

I was young and never stopped to think that if I didn't have these simple forms of support, my life would have been so chaotic and unstable. I started being kinder to my family. I was more appreciative of the little things, and Tony brought that out in me. Tony did not have that kind of love in his life—the type of unconditional love that allows you to make mistakes without the permanent scars of judgment. Tony did not have stability or rules. He was almost eighteen and didn't know what direction he wanted to go in life. I didn't either, but I had guidance and support from my parents, who would do anything to ensure I succeeded. I figured everyone had that in life but learning about Tony made me realize I was wrong.

I've always been attracted to broken people because my empathy draws people in and helps them feel safe. Tony and I got very comfortable and talked about intimate things, too. At that age, I didn't even know what sex was or what it represented, let alone how it affected me emotionally. Tony was the first person I could even remotely get comfortable talking about intimacy with. He sparked this fire in me that I never knew I had. We would get on the phone, and after our regular deep talks, we'd wonder what it would feel like to kiss each other. He lived many hours away, and neither could travel that far, so this was all a fantasy. We never talked about a relationship; I never wanted that. I assumed he never wanted that, either. We were just each other's company and relief from loneliness. There was romance to it.

He spoke to me about his ex-girlfriend and how toxic she was. He loved her, but things were always intense and rocky with them. They constantly got into heated arguments and were unhappy, so they took a break. Even through his hurt, he was a hopeless romantic and said sweet words to me, like, "The sound of your voice makes me happy." The wittiness in our conversations drove me mad in the most erotic way. At sixteen, erotic was not in my vocabulary, but now I see that is precisely what it was.

It wasn't common in the Indian culture to have the "sex talk." Intimacy was not something we talked about with our parents, and it felt uncomfortable to bring it up. To this day, I haven't seen my parents kiss on the lips. It's safe to say that talking about something as intimate as sex is not a topic we bring up in our homes. So, I admired Tony's intelligence and maturity, and it was a turn-on. I loved when we would use our "baby voices" with each other and how he'd say, "The way you laugh is so cute; it gives me butterflies." Those are the types of words that got my stomach in knots, the kind that you don't want to untie. The kind that makes you giddy inside and brings emotion to your eyes. I was starting to learn that affirmations were my love language.

In school, I would daydream about him and think of the deep tones of his voice. I would close my eyes and picture us together. This was when reality hit. I looked nothing like the person that he was envisioning being with. When I would think about us, I was Deepti he was with and not Jessica. When he would think about me, he saw her. The thought of that deeply saddened me, and I wanted to stop what I was doing at those moments. Pretending to be someone I wasn't was exhausting.

One day at school, I remember someone calling out the name Jessica, and I flinched. I thought someone was talking to me. It was fucking with my head. It made me anxious, and I knew it was not right anymore. That night I came home, I didn't talk to Tony. I locked myself in my room, journaled, listened to music, and escaped into my mind.

The next day, Tony disappeared. I don't know what

happened, but I didn't get one text, instant message, or call from him. That one day became a week and then a month. I was sad and depressed. I didn't realize how much he had added to my life until then. But in a way, a part of me was relieved. I didn't have to tell him the truth, and the memory of us stays intact for what we created it to be. His ghosting me, paired with the feeling of guilt, was enough to convince me to stop being Jessica. It was doing too much harm, and I recognized that. I started to erase her existence from my memory. I didn't log in as her for months.

I continued with life as if it had never happened. I got back into the routine of going to school and tennis practice. I was happy with the friendships I had in real life again. I would help my mom cook. I enjoyed doing that with her. She loved the company and appreciated that I was spending more time outside instead of being locked in my room. I would play games with my sister and pretend to read with her. I say pretend because I did not like to read; I liked the *idea* of reading. On the other hand, my sister, Divya, would read book after book. I admired that about her and saw how maturely and beautifully she was growing up. I hadn't recognized that before; I always thought of her as a baby. I was too wrapped up in my thoughts to see what was happening around me.

Another school year was starting. A few months into the semester, I was reminded of Tony as I was watching a television show and noticed that the actor in it looked just like him. I am not sure why I thought of him just then, but I decided to log back in as Jessica. I wanted to check if he had reached out to me, and my curious mind overpowered my will. To my surprise, he hadn't messaged me at all. Oddly, for some reason, I thought I would have a message, but I never got it. I was disappointed, but in a way, I'm glad that I didn't. It would have prevented me from moving forward and becoming Deepti again.

It did get me reminiscing about our conversations. I thought, *Had things gotten bad for him at home? Did something happen with his ex-girlfriend?* I hoped he was doing well and had moved on to something exciting. I had no idea what had happened. I realized that Tony was still a stranger to me in many ways, and to be honest, in that moment, I was happy this was the case. I was too scared of the idea of someone getting this close to me.

I'd only watched romance in movies, and that kind of love was always something I'd wanted. However, I realized this wasn't true love. He didn't even know what I really looked like. I had been lying to him the whole time, and that is certainly not a great starting point for a relationship. I decided that this had been for the best and that I needed to continue living my *real* life and not be disrupted.

My body image issues continued throughout the rest of high school. I always wore cardigans or sweatshirts over any outfit because it made me feel more comfortable. In addition to the sweaters protecting me from the Antarctic temperatures the school had set on the thermostat, the sweaters also hid my body from being seen. In classes, the seats were set up in rows, and I despised being seated in the front. I was self-conscious about the other students being able to see me. I even thought twice about reaching into my backpack to grab something because movement attracted eyes. I sat extremely still in the classes where I felt most uncomfortable. There were only two classes where I felt this way, and in the others, I was free because I sat in the back. I remember thinking how blessed I was to have a last name that ended in "V." I was last in line for most things based on our alphabetical last name placements.

There was one class I dreaded the most. It triggered anxiety in me, and for the right reasons. My English teacher wanted to mix it up and would randomly arrange us into a seating assignment. I was seated at the front of the classroom. The worst part was sitting next to the mean, popular cheerleaders. I rarely spoke to them to avoid letting them know of my existence. This day was different. The teacher made us do a group exercise in randomly selected clusters with the people around us. Of course, my worst nightmare came true, and I was paired with the meanest girl in the school.

All the cheerleaders were gorgeous, thin, and vain girls who rarely studied. To be fair, this is what I assumed at the time. In my mind, they were perfect, not realizing that I had beautiful traits of my own that they didn't possess.

We are all different, with unique gifts to show the world. It's easy to emphasize all the wrong things about ourselves, but that's part of the maturing process as the brain is still learning and growing. I put them on a pedestal because I valued their beauty and likability, which made them seem intimidating to me. I gave them power with my thoughts. The control was within me to see that they were not how I portrayed them in my mind, but I didn't know how to change that thought pattern at the time. The group exercise went surprisingly well; they even laughed at my jokes. I felt happy leaving the classroom that day. The next day, however, was not as satisfying.

Next day in English class, one of the girls pointed out and said, "Didn't you wear that sweatshirt yesterday?" I always kept a sweatshirt in my locker as an emotional and physical blanket. This comment felt like a word punch. I tried to let it roll off my back. I wasn't about to take my sweatshirt off. I didn't care what they said. This was the first jab they took that semester. The second was worse. They said I smelled like curry. They didn't know that it was vegetable biryani, the most delicious meal ever. Indian food has a powerful aroma that occasionally lingers, even on my clothes. Again, this was another comment that I let slide. What else would I do? Say something back? That was not in my nature. I hated confrontation, so I let them say what they wanted and pretended like I didn't even hear it. The bullying from them got worse as the year went on. It never got physical, but it was tiny word daggers on a repeated basis that left impressionable scars.

Winter break could not come soon enough. Almost a week before we left for vacation, the girls were in an especially mean mood. They were joking with each other and making snarky remarks about the other students in class. They were having fun being sarcastic with some guys who were the typical popular kids. They played sports and had lots of friends. One of the girls joked about one of them dating me, which became a huge ordeal. He yelled, "That's disgusting," to which the girls laughed.

I think you can guess how I felt.

Then, one responded, "Yeah, I couldn't imagine having such a fat girlfriend." This comment hit deep for me. It stabbed me a little harder than all of the other jabs. I remember going to the bathroom and crying after that class.

Externally, I always pretended to be okay in front of other people. Internally, the words were stuck on repeat playing over and over. I didn't know how to take the record off the phonograph; it was stuck. These words triggered me deeply.

It was not long after that day that my battle with bulimia returned. It was triggered by my circumstances. There were many long periods of time that I didn't overindulge in food because I was distracted by being Jessica. When my focus shifted back to the realities of my own life, I turned to food. I loved eating and found so much happiness in it, but I hated myself afterward, so I would force myself to throw it up. It made me feel better ... for a short while. It's fascinating to look back now and see how much my negative bingeing and purging cycles were connected to how I was feeling about myself. When I was pretending to be Jessica and having a great time flirting with Tony, I found that my bingeing was less common. But coming back to being Deepti and hearing repeated criticisms about my appearance caused all of the unhealthy thoughts I had about myself to return. This triggered me to reactivate Jessica. I longed to be able to connect with somebody and share my feelings. I longed to escape. And then, one day, I found my perfect distraction. His name was Landon.

Landon was exactly my type. He had a dominating personality and took a considerable interest in talking to Jessica. I loved his enthusiasm and high energy. He was very generous with his compliments and made me feel good about myself again. His parents were easygoing and let him have a car and lots of freedom. He was fantastic with words; we could talk about anything and everything for hours. Sometimes, the conversations were as simple as what we were watching on television, and other times, the conversations were in-depth thoughts about our romantic feelings toward each other. He listened to country music and always sent me sweet loving lyrics from his favorite bands. I loved listening to music, so this gesture was heartwarming. After a short while of chatting online, he was quick to ask to hang out, which made me realize that this relationship was not like the last time. I couldn't put myself in this position. After a little while, it was hard to come up with excuses not to meet. I knew I had to end it. I was just looking for a distraction because of my negative experiences at school. There had to be an end anyway. Landon was short-lived, and it was getting too real. I decided to stop Jessica from resurfacing.

School restarted, and time was flying. I remember calculus was my favorite class because I was good at it. Math excited me because there was always a solution and a correct answer to every problem. It was logical and to the point. The other reason I liked calculus was that I sat right next to my crush. We will call him Trent.

Trent was the sweetest. You'd never know that he was a jock based on his personality. He had so much depth and the emotional intelligence I sought in people. He was flirty with me but not in a passionate way; it was just his underlying personality. I never stood a chance with him romantically. I longed to talk to Trent outside of calculus class where he could see the real me, but I decided that was never going to happen. My crush on him turned into something more robust and obsessive. I waited all day for the next calculus class to begin just so I could see him and talk to him. It was as if every day for forty-five minutes, I was injecting a dose of Trent into my bloodstream. I was feeling euphoric about him.

One day something came over me, and I wanted to talk to Trent as Jessica. I longed for him to want to speak to me in greater depth. Jessica took over me once again, and I sought out Trent on Myspace. He responded quickly as I had hoped. Talking to Trent was the easiest thing I'd ever done. He was kind and caring. Unlike all of my previous online connections, this one felt extra special because I had a physical, real-life crush on him as well. We connected quickly; I know a big part of that was because he was physically attracted to Jessica. I suppressed that thought entirely so I could justify my actions. I told myself it was okay when I knew deep down that it wasn't.

Trent wanted to go to prom with me that year. I said, "Yes," just to please him and move on from the subject. Prom was over two months away, so I thought I would be able to buy some time to continue to talk to him. But Trent was eager and excited to go to prom with Jessica, and so he began making preparations. Within a week of Jessica saying yes to going to prom, Trent told me that his mom had already bought him a tux. My heart sank. *Oh no*, I thought. *This has gone too far*.

I had to tell Trent I couldn't go to prom, and he didn't take it well. He was upset that his mom had spent a lot of money to get his tux for that day. He was also clearly disappointed. I felt awful. After that moment, I had to stop talking to Trent. I could no longer keep going with this act. It had real-life consequences that I could not control. My intention was never to hurt anyone, but I realized with Trent that my actions were causing a lot of pain and sadness.

After a month of no contact with Trent as Jessica, I received a phone call. It was an unknown number, but there was a voicemail. When I heard it, my entire body felt numb. It was the police. Anxiety and fear showered my whole body.

I ignored the voicemail initially because I didn't know what to do at that moment. I needed some time to think. What was I going to tell my parents? How would I deal with the judgment I would get from my classmates? How do I apologize? The officer didn't say what the call was regarding, but I knew. What else could it be?

My parents had already found out by the time I got home from school that day. They were never home before me from work. This time after tennis practice, they were practically waiting for me at the front door. They asked millions of questions, and I just stood in silence, trying to find the words to justify any of my wrongdoings. I could see the worry in my parents' eyes. They weren't even thinking of my punishment; they were sad that I had done something like this. I had to tell them everything about Jessica and finally be honest. We were asked to talk to the detective the next day, which was the scariest day of my life. I knew I had disappointed my parents and was about to face the repercussions of the biggest mistake I would ever make.

My parents have always been kind and compassionate. They showed tough love sometimes, but they believed that it would push me to be better in life. They were always kind to every person they'd meet. They had hearts of gold, and people—even strangers—remembered them for their thoughtfulness and love. The detective working with us felt that in them too. He could sense their worry as much as I did. Everything was laid out on the table, and the truth was right in front of us. I couldn't do anything but apologize and explain that I knew it was wrong and nothing could fix it.

You might be wondering how the detective found out about me. I wondered the same thing. They had reverse looked up my number and found my dad's name. It didn't match that of a Jessica. Now, get ready for my pivotal moment. The detective I was working with was also in communication with Jessica's family. This frightened me even more. I continued to emphatically express my stand-point and show that I was not a bad person. I was lost, confused, and acted in error. I was not trying to justify my actions but own them and show that I was sorry.

I didn't realize it then, but I know it was my luckiest day. It was a blessing that her family showed me grace. They saw the human side of me. Even though they were upset, they knew I was not ill-intended. With my parents' warmth and my willingness to understand the severity of the situa-tion, they let us go. This allowed my parents to deal with me on their own. Jessica's family understood that I was just a teen, and they didn't want to ruin my chances for a good future. The detective believed I would change my ways and never do this again. And he was right. My interaction with that detective is the reason why I am a different person today. He taught me that mistakes could be made in life, but that does not mean life ends. Jessica's family's compassion for me was the catalyst that led me to create a permanent change within myself.

It is an embarrassing and shameful feeling to share my mistakes with you. It invokes a fear inside of me that makes me want to run. What are people going to think? Will they change their perception of me? Will I be able to live with the judgment? Am I ready for haters?

When I have racing thoughts of anxiety over sharing this dark moment of my life, a quote from Meg Cabot, author of *The Princess Diaries*, comes to mind:

> "Courage is not the absence of fear, but rather the judgment that something is more important than fear. The brave may not live forever, but the cautious do not live at all. You'll be traveling the road between who you think you are and who you want to be. The key is to allow yourself to make the journey."

That quote is more meaningful to me now than when I first heard it in 2001. I feel that sharing this part of my past with you will have a more profound positive impact than hiding it. It will allow those who felt like me at sixteen to pause and take a step back to realize they shouldn't make the same mistakes I did. Being someone else never fixes any problem. It also allows those who are quick to judge actions like mine to see it from a different perspective.

Anger is usually the first response. Judgment is the next. We must have the courage to look inward and address what is truly making us feel sad and insecure. The journey to loving ourselves is an ongoing process with many ups and downs. This was one of the lower points in my life, but in many ways, it was just the beginning of my journey to becoming my authentic self.

LIBERATING A CAGED BIRD

"Some birds are not meant to be caged.
Their feathers are just too bright."
– MORGAN FREEMAN IN
SHAWSHANK REDEMPTION

Not surprisingly, I lost all my privileges after I got caught catfishing. No phone, no friend outings, no computer access, and no closing my bedroom door unless it was to change. Honestly, I was thrilled with that, considering the consequences could've been more severe. It was a wake-up call. I needed to change my behavior and my mindset.

That 2009 summer of limited freedom was transformational for me. Because I didn't have any other distractions, I was able to focus my energy inward and decided to change my eating habits. I became more active, and when I craved conversations, I would go to my sister, Divya.

Divya and I bonded that summer. We would play tennis, challenge each other to board games, ride bikes, and share Razor scooters around the neighborhood. It's funny how for all my years prior, I thought of Divya as just my baby sister; what I didn't see was that I had a friend in her all along. It helped me to have her, my family, and my dog, Pixel, around me during this time of healing. My parents didn't continuously punish me for my mistake; they saw a change in me and my attitude. I'd like to think they saw the light in me again. I was more present and engaged with them—I was no longer locking myself in my bedroom for hours on end. I began to feel better about myself, not only because I started losing weight but also because I stopped my bingeing and purging cycle. I became more physically active, which in turn released the serotonin that made me happier. It showed.

By the end of a pivotal summer of working on myself, I was very much looking forward to my senior year of high school. Finally, I could spend time with kids my age, and they could see the new me. I found myself much more interested in school when my semester started. I liked my classes and was determined to study and do well. Playing on the varsity tennis team gave me so much joy. I loved my tennis girls. I appreciated my tennis conferences on the weekends because it meant I could start spending some time outside of the house. My parents began to trust me again because of my changed habits. I was growing as a person. I accepted that I would not go out too much with friends, and my parents eased up and allowed me to interact with them. I was home by 10:00 p.m., and this didn't bother me anymore. I didn't fight it. I simply accepted it for what it was.

Graduation and senior prom were coming up, and I was

ecstatic. I was also terrified because I hadn't yet found a date. At this point, I felt good about my body, grades, and relationships. I learned to drive, and my parents let me take Sunny's car whenever he was away at college. I got accepted into some colleges and picked one—Bradley University. I was in the best head space I had been in a long time.

One night, Kendall had a brilliant idea for my prom date. She suggested that one of her friends, whom I'd hung out with multiple times, could be a potential option. He knew me, he was kind, and we had fun hanging out in groups. There was no romantic connection, so this made things more comfortable. One evening, we asked him together, and he quickly said yes. I was so happy. The last year of high school was memorable, even though I was grounded for most of it. That was the exact punishment I needed. It was as if I had to go through a difficult time to learn to appreciate the small things in life.

Senior prom was one of the most fun times of my high school experience. I bought a beautiful dress, and I felt like a princess. The dress was a light blue evening gown that still hangs in my parents' closet today. I met up with all my best friends and their dates for photos before the ceremony, and my parents were there to see us off too. After taking pictures, all the parents left, and we headed to an Italian dinner.

After dinner, we parked in the school lot before heading inside for the dance. I called my parents to let them know I had made it safely to school. As I was on the phone, John pulled out a warm bottle of Patrón Tequila he stole from his dad's liquor cabinet. Everyone was taking swigs, and he handed the bottle to me. I paused for a moment to think about whether to accept the offer or not, as I had never drunk alcohol before. In mid-conversation with my mom, I said, "One second, Mom," and took a swig of tequila. I then went back on the phone as if it was nothing.

That summer seemed to fly by quickly. Kendall stayed the night at my house a lot. It was easier for my parents to trust this. One day, they were gone to work, and Kendall was over. I went to the basement to grab something, and by the time I returned, I didn't see her in the living room where I'd left her. I went upstairs searching and found her in my parents' bedroom. It was so odd that she was up there. I can't recall what she said she was doing there. I valued her friendship even though Kendall tended to lie. This time was a little different.

That night when my parents returned home, they noticed money missing from their dresser drawer. I hadn't taken it; I didn't need money. My parents always bought me anything and everything I ever needed. So, I knew it was Kendall, and her suspicious nature when I caught her in my parents' bedroom all made sense to me. I began to change my perception of her. I didn't like confrontation, so I didn't accuse her, but I just kept this knowledge in the back of my mind. After that, I was cautious of her and limited my interactions. Summer was coming to an end anyway, and it was time to go our separate ways.

When September came, it was time for me to head to college. I was excited about starting this next stage of life but wondered if my idea of going to college was a little skewed. I wasn't really thinking about excelling in my classes and impressing my professors—instead, I was thinking about the new freedom I would have living outside of my parents' house.

It was an emotional day for me when my parents helped me move into my dorm room. I noticed how carefully they set everything up for me and took me shopping to get groceries for my little fridge. They so lovingly took care of me, and now, I realized, I had to care for myself. In the excitement of what I was gaining, I didn't quite grasp the love and comfort I was losing. Within an hour of them leaving, I already missed them.

Bradley University was a small school, and I liked that aspect. My roommate was randomly chosen, and I was perfectly fine with that because I got along with most people. I remember her being dominant and knowing precisely what she wanted for her career—to be a nurse. I was the opposite. I had no clue what I wanted to do with my life. I honestly just wanted to live life to the fullest. I assumed everything would fall into place.

The first night was called "freshmen night." The school organized a fun event, but it was a notorious night for parties. All the fraternities threw a party, and all the freshmen got to go wild. It was a way to welcome the first-year students. That night was my indoctrination into party life. If only I remembered how much "jungle juice" I drank.

I decided to major in communication because I always wanted to go into journalism. I thought it was the easiest subject, and I was already good at it. I had no idea that it would entail so much learning. Even though I was outgoing with my friends, the idea of standing up in a classroom full of students and speaking was terrifying. Classes and homework became such a chore.

I landed a job at State Farm during my senior year of high school. This job crept into my first year of college. So, every Friday night, I would take a bus home so that I could work over the weekend at this internship. It took a toll on me, so I decided to quit mid-semester. I was free from being cooped up at my parents' home now, and all I wanted to do was hang out with friends and party.

My relationship with my dorm roommate started to go downhill as we crept into the fall of my first semester. I could see her energy shifted, and she wasn't spending much time in the room as she once did. We were close at the start, but I could feel her withdraw from me. She prioritized other friends and hung out with our mutual friends without me. To this day, I am not sure what exactly happened. But it did hit my ego, and I started to pull back.

I started to fall into a slightly depressed state of mind and stopped eating. I noticed my weight loss from this, and I loved it. But, not eating made me even more depressed, and at that time, I didn't connect the dots that these were interconnected. I became shy and introspective. Fears crept into my mind and ignited my insecurities even further. So, I did whatever I had to do, not to cross paths with my roommate and would sleep in my friends' rooms to avoid her entirely. I started going out more, avoiding classwork, and drinking to cope. I was not adjusting well. It didn't help that I missed my family and home. I also realized I needed my alone time as much as I socialized. My social meter had a limit, and it required an occasional recharge.

I introduced myself at parties as "deep like the ocean, tea like the drink" because everyone was always confused with my name. Because Bradley is a small college, by the second semester of freshman year, most of the students in my classes knew me; I was unique. This didn't mean I still didn't have insecurities. I had more than ever before. I was surrounded by beautiful girls and boys who liked these beautiful girls. It was never me. I was always the friend who tagged along on dates or joined groups but never romantically had someone in my life.

I was tired of going unnoticed. Everyone loved my personality, but I always knew my physical appearance was what kept guys from romantically thinking of me. I started hitting the gym with the girlfriends I made on my floor. It was then that I realized how much I loved working out. It was almost like therapy to me and made me feel so alive. It was the one thing I could control. I was so thankful for my beautiful friends who had the same mindset to get into shape. I was learning from them to be more independent and make better choices. I hadn't realized that with freedom comes a responsibility to myself. I knew I wasn't making the proper choices to become a better person. I was going out too much and wasn't concentrating on the education my parents were paying copious amounts for. I knew that I was smart, but I was not acting like it. That semester, I failed a class. This was a wake-up call, the one I needed to get my mind right.

My parents were upset that I had wasted so much time and money just to fail. It wasn't that I was dumb; I simply didn't want to put in the effort. I didn't want to be told what to do anymore. I wanted to live life in my way. But my parents had other plans for me. They put a lot of pressure on me to change my major and pick a career path. I still had no idea what I wanted to do.

The summer back home after my first year in college was a tough one for me. I was back to living with my parents' strict rules. I went into another depression. All I wanted to do was be with my friends, but all I got to do was stay home with my family. At least I had my sister at home. We had grown closer in my last year of high school, and I looked forward to spending time with her. While I was a rebel, Divya always followed the rules. Despite this, oddly, I looked up to her. She wasn't always calm and quiet; she had many stern opinions. She challenged my line of thinking, and I think that's what I loved about her most. She was her own person and had a solid moral compass. Divya helped me move out of the depression that summer without even knowing it. I never let her know any of this at the time.

My sophomore year brought new adventures. I decided to change my major to psychology. The subject fascinated me. Learning the behaviors and mindsets of people and understanding the way the brain works was intriguing. I also got a new roommate, and she was perfect. Not only was she gorgeous, but she was also kind and free-spirited. She complemented my personality. We became best friends and spent all our time together. She always attracted a lot of attention from boys because of her extroverted and charming personality. She also put a lot of care into her studies which inspired me to do the same. I knew I couldn't let my parents down anymore. I had to study, I had to be mindful, and it helped that I surrounded myself with people who were doing the same thing. Don't get me wrong; we still had the time of our lives socially, but we kept up with our school responsibilities.

When Halloween rolled around, my friends from my

hometown invited me to go to the University of Illinois to celebrate. This school was huge, and they did Halloween the same way: a massive celebration and no chance I'd miss it. If I had let my parents know, they would never have let me go, so I just tagged along with some friends. They didn't need to know everything I did. I mean, I was almost twenty years old at this point. Of course, drinking was involved, and we were fraternity hopping.

I walked into one of the frat houses and immediately noticed a guy staring at me. Honestly, I had no idea what his real face looked like to this day because he was dressed as a mime for Halloween, and his face was covered entirely in white paint. He beelined to me quickly within seconds of being in the house. I was a little tipsy but was along for the ride. We took some shots, ended up upstairs, and kissed within fifteen minutes.

My phone was in my back pocket during this entire interaction. Then, the worst and most bizarre thing I could have ever imagined happened. I accidently butt-dialed my mom. (The lesson here is, don't put your parents on speed dial when you know you're clumsy and make mistakes!) I'm not exactly sure what my mom heard, but since I was not responding to her, she freaked out. While still having the phone connected, my parents made their way to Bradley to pick me up. They didn't know that I was not there. In retrospect, I laugh at this story because what are the chances of doing this to myself and getting in trouble again? It was as if the universe was punishing me for stepping out of line by lying to my parents about where I was and what I was doing. After about fifteen minutes of my mom being on the line, I looked at my phone, and my heart sank into my stomach. This was it. My parents would kill me. They would pull me out of school and ship me back to India.

Even though I was a young adult, I was terrified of my mom. She was so strict, and I knew I had disappointed her again. I quickly hung up the phone and frantically went looking for my friends. I hadn't realized how long I was gone, but my friends searched the entire house for me. They were going into each room to find me, relieved when we reunited. I told them the situation and saw my mom calling me a million times repeatedly after I hung up the phone. In a panic, we ran out of the frat house and started walking to my friend's place.

I knew I had to answer the phone, and I was unsure what was waiting for me on the other end. When I answered, my mom immediately started yelling at me that she was so worried. I didn't expect this reaction as I was not thinking about the situation from her perspective. I always expected her to be angry, but I could sense she was just concerned and worried about me at this moment. She wanted to ensure I was okay, which made me realize that maybe I had been selfish over the years. Perhaps I hadn't considered everything I had put my parents through.

My mom told me they were coming to pick me up, and I asked, "From where?"

She said, "We're five minutes away from Bradley."

I had to break it to them that I was not there. I'm unsure how this made them feel, but I told them where I was. She hung up the phone, and this completely shook me. There was no chance of freedom any longer. I looked to my friends and immediately said, "I need to sober up."

Although in the back of my mind, I knew there was no chance of that happening.

Ten minutes later, I got another call from my mom. All she said to me was, tell me where you are; we are coming to pick you up. In a shaky voice, I told them, and they made the hour-and-a-half drive to me. When they picked me up, I remember how drunk I was. I laid down in the backseat and didn't say a word. They also didn't say a word to me.

The following day, my dad said, "I'm taking you back to school." This completely surprised me because I was sure there was no going back. My mom didn't speak to me at all that morning. My dad barely said anything to me during the car ride back to school. He dropped me off and said, "Be careful and stay safe." And to this day, we have not spoken about that incident, not even once.

After that eventful night, it was like something awakened inside of me. As you can tell, this was a reoccurring theme with me. I would make a mistake and realize I needed to ponder my actions. I'd make some moves to adjust my behavior until I made the next mistake, and the cycle started over again. I was driven more than ever to succeed this time around. I was still going to have fun, but to do that, I needed to concentrate and put effort into my life's direction. Even if I was a little rocky following through on my new commitment, the intention was certainly there. I was finally starting to succeed in my classes. I had great friends who supported me and understood me.

Also, that semester, my friend's brother introduced me to weed. I had no idea what this was when I first came across it, and soon, I realized I loved it. I felt more in control when I was high; it was much different from alcohol.

Alcohol was inhibiting and would make me blackout sometimes, which was a scary feeling. So, this felt safer, and I
loved getting high with friends and having chill nights.
Overall, college life was moving in a good direction.

The time came to start thinking about where and with
whom I'd live come junior year. It was time to move out of
the dorms and find my own place. As much as I loved my
current roommate, I decided to move in with the three girlfriends I met and was still close to from freshman year. I
was sad that I would no longer live with my best friend and
roommate, but it felt right because I didn't know her other
friends well. Not to the level that I knew mine. They were a
different group of people, and I still loved them just the
same. It did feel like I was choosing sides. This started to
create a little tension with my current roommate, which
saddened me. I simply couldn't please everyone.

One day, we went to an apartment party, and the trajectory of my college experience changed entirely. That night,
I met who would become my college—and first official—
boyfriend (let's call him Jeremy), who completely lit up my
whole world. This is precisely what I had desired since I
was fifteen, someone that showed me love and affection.
Someone that I could call my own. He went to a community
college in the city and was a little older than me. That night
at the party, we ended up smoking weed and talking all
night long. After hanging out a few times, he asked me to
be his girlfriend. This was the best feeling in the world and
the perfect way to end the semester.

I got a paid internship at a cable company and started
working there full-time that summer. This internship was
such a blessing because I could move in early to my new

place for junior year, and all three of my new roommates would be with me. They were all working too, so I didn't have any FOMO. This was the first time where I was able to continue living out of my parents' house during the summer, and I was grateful for the freedom.

Jeremy and I spent all our free time together that summer. He was into art, and his fascination with it mesmerized me. I learned then that I loved having a partner who was creative and passionate about their own interests. Jeremy was a sweet person, but he was not perfect. The more time we spent together, the more I noticed he would go through waves of unpredictable emotion. It didn't help that he and I had different personalities. I was full of energy and up for an adventure, and he was often anxious and wanted to stay in and play video games.

One day he told me that he was diagnosed with depression and mentioned he was taking medication to manage it. I was learning more about this condition in my psychology classes and could also relate to it because I had had my own bouts of feeling depressed in the past. I knew that reminding someone who has a mental illness that they're not alone is one of the most important things to do. I made a point to let Jeremy know that I was here for him. I never judged him for wanting to stay in when I wanted to go out, and I tried to keep positive, even when things got tough.

I wanted to make Jeremy happy because, at that time, he was the source of my happiness. And so, eventually, when I could see he was getting upset with me going out so much, I started canceling plans to ease his anxiety. I would stay home, and we would spend hours in my room alone together. My friends started to see a shift in me; I wasn't hanging out with them as much as I had been during the summer.

When classes started again, I became very close to my roommate, Laura. She was one of my closest friends and still is to this day. I feel like you go through seasons of having different close friends when you're with them. And then life happens, and you are on two different paths. When you live with someone, you naturally get close to them, which was the case with most of my roommates. When I think back on all the memories now, I realize that I would have never made it through the last two years of college without Laura. She added vibrance and color to my life, and we did everything together. We always joke that it's because we are both air signs. Astrology says Aquarius and Libra energies mesh very well together. She was into fashion and helped inspire me with my style.

We always had an absolute blast together. Guys would obsess over her. As I reflect on my teen and adult life, I see a pattern I didn't know I had at that time. I realized that I would always notice when guys pined over my girlfriends. I can now see that I continuously watched how guys viewed my friends because I craved that kind of attention for myself. It was almost like I was vicariously experiencing how it felt to be desired through seeing my friends experience it.

Laura introduced me to the raver world and electronic dance music (EDM); it had me hypnotized. *This* was my kind of music. We started going to EDM music festivals and shows regularly. Jeremy was not thrilled about this because I was now spending more time with Laura than with him. I tried to get him to come out with us, but he always decided to stay behind. He said he didn't mind that I was without him on some weekend nights.

Laura also had a boyfriend, so she was off with him. Sometimes we would do double dates and hang out in groups. Jeremy wasn't too keen on that either because he often gets socially tired. Sometimes others' energies drained him. I understood that feeling and never argued for him to be different.

I liked Jeremy's witty, artistic introverted personality. It balanced my extroverted nature. We enjoyed our alone time together, but I'd often find that I would suppress my personality to please him. I never realized that breaking up over it was an option. He was my first boyfriend, and I was figuring it out. All I knew was that I didn't want to lose him. We started spending even more time together, and I decided to stay with him instead of going out. This codependency was getting stronger by the day. I didn't want to leave his side, and he didn't want to leave mine.

Throughout this part of my relationship with Jeremy, I realized I was starting to lose interest in school again. The classes were getting more challenging with each passing semester, and I had to put in extra work to maintain my grades, and this didn't excite me. Jeremy wasn't in school at that point, and I found myself latching onto his lifestyle instead of putting in the time I knew I should've been on my studies. I felt afraid to do my own thing for fear that I may lose him.

Somehow, I powered through the semesters of that year, juggling my relationship and my friends. But I was becoming increasingly codependent in my relationship. Jeremy and I were always together when I wasn't in school.

I started spending less time in the common areas of our house with my roommates and more time alone with him in my room.

That summer, I got a job in Social Services, and I loved it. While working there, I realized just how much helping others brought me joy. I decided that I wanted to be a therapist. Ironically, while I often liked to ignore my own problems, I really liked helping others solve theirs. The little kids I got to know from my job that summer became such an important part of my life. These kids had been abused by their caretakers and were no longer allowed to live with them. For the parents to regain sole custody, they had to go through government-approved classes and go to court to prove they were ready for sole custody again. We all know how long it takes to go through something in court. These parents had to prove they were making enough substantial changes to provide their kids with the right type of love and home environment.

During this long process, they still had the right to visit with their kids. That's where I came into the picture. I picked the kids up from their foster homes and took them to see their parents. This had to be supervised because Social Services didn't trust the parents alone with their kids. The kids I worked with had sad stories. One of them was burned for acting up; some were beaten. Others didn't have guardians attending to them, and they were neglected or abandoned for days. These kids were so special to me. They needed love, and I had so much of it for them.

As my senior year rolled around, I realized it was time to consider what I wanted to do after graduation. All my friends had already started to know what they wanted and were getting job offers. I felt a little lost. I chatted with my advisers and realized that I wasn't fond of the research aspect of psychology. If I pursued it, I would have to go to graduate school and put in a lot more effort in a structured institution. The lingering thought of continuing and pursuing higher education was over-whelming. I wanted to work, even if it was just as a bartender. I was happier making money than I was spending it to learn. This was a bit of a backward mental-ity, but at that time, I didn't want to do research and go through the process of becoming a psychologist—even though I loved the subject.

After careful consideration, I decided to add business management to my degree. My parents and brother were already in technology, so adding informational analysis into my classes felt like a no-brainer. It was almost as if it was in my blood. I grasped it quickly and liked learning about it. Since I was adding these classes into my curriculum so late in the game, I had to take some extra courses to graduate in time with my class. This meant I had to quit my job at Social Services so I could focus. This was heartbreaking because the kids I worked with relied on me. I was their only constant for many months, and I didn't want to leave them hanging. But it was time for me to move on, and it felt like the right move. I knew they would be in good hands with another intern.

I often think about those kids and how they must be doing. They were such a big part of my life and taught me so many important life lessons. They taught me to appre-ciate everything I had taken for granted, including my parents and their unconditional love. They helped put into perspective the sacrifices my parents made so my siblings and I could have a better life.

Around this time, I realized that my interest in my relationship with Jeremy was fading. However, I cared about him too much to end the relationship, and our codependency was at an all-time high. Often, when we weren't together, at least one of us would feel anxious, and this would reinforce an anxious attachment style. We relied too much on each other for happiness that we never really stopped to consider if we were happy on our own.

Even though I saw that my relationship with Jeremy wasn't healthy, I valued his company. He was my first boyfriend, and I loved him. I was close with his parents, and we would visit them often, so it made me apprehensive to think about not spending time together in the future.

Graduation was approaching, which meant a new start was on the horizon. It was time for me to branch out of Peoria. I spent the last four years there, and I was outgrowing it. I needed to leave to explore more of what the world had to offer. Even with our challenges, I knew I would miss Jeremy when I moved away, so we decided to make a long-distance relationship work.

I moved back home with my parents and never even told them I was in a relationship. I was too scared to talk to them about boys and kept that part of my life wholly hidden from them. I would lie, say I was spending time with Laura, and go to his place instead. I didn't feel good about these lies, and they started to add up. I was living a double life again, one my parents had no clue about. As they read this, they might find it shocking to know all the details too. This was the easiest way to live my life on my terms at this point. I didn't want them to prevent me from going to see him, so it was easier to fabricate the truth. I always used Laura as an excuse to find time for Jeremy. But slowly, I was starting to realize that Jeremy and I were drifting apart.

This was also the summer I started to take care of my body more than ever before. I had never looked better. Taking care of myself and giving my body the proper nourishment skyrocketed my confidence. I wasn't drinking alcohol as much now because I was at home, which definitely helped me feel more present. I worked out every day and fed my body fruits and vegetables. I realized that you operate at a higher vibrational frequency when you start to take care of your body, mind, and soul. People notice. I began to attract attention from other guys for the first time. I felt comfortable in my skin and was proud of myself. My confidence levels motivated my consistency. Even my old high school classmates started to notice and take an interest in me.

I went to a party that summer where there were many attractive men. One specific man caught my eye. He was exactly my type: six foot two and had a soccer body with a piercing. I was captivated. But I was still in a relationship with Jeremy. I judged myself for being so into this other guy, and it didn't help that I knew he was attracted to me. We spent the whole party flirting and talking. Since we were drinking, we both decided to stay the night at our friend's place. He got one couch, and I got the other. He tried to lean in to kiss me multiple times, but I denied the kiss. I wanted to kiss him so badly, but I could never cheat on Jeremy. I was proud of my integrity and self-control. I was never going to be that girl. But this sparked something in me. I knew at that moment that I had to end my relationship. We had outgrown each other, and it was time to move on.

Meeting new people made me realize how different Jeremy and I were. I wanted to move to Chicago and start a new life, and he was still stagnant where he was. We were hanging on by a thread, and moving to a long-distance relationship only highlighted how poor our communication was. Jeremy rarely texted or called me anymore. His work hours were sporadic, and our schedules didn't complement each other. Our paths were splitting, which saddened me, but I had to have the courage to let go of the codependency. Just because a relationship starts to feel familiar doesn't mean it's healthy. It also doesn't mean it's right for you. As sad as this break-up was for both of us, I knew a bright future was ahead of me, and new experiences were waiting to be lived. There was a new beginning on the horizon.

IMAGINE THE FUTURE

"Don't make friends who are comfortable
to be with. Make friends who will
force you to lever yourself up."
– THOMAS J. WATSON.

Graduating from college was a significant milestone for me. I had been through many ups and downs during those years and discovered a lot about myself. I've always been someone who listened to my heart to decide what is right for me, which sometimes leads to feelings of loneliness, especially when friends and family question my choices. Sure, I hadn't always made perfect choices—who has?—but they were *my* choices, and I loved that independence.

My mission now was to develop my life as an adult. I knew that this next chapter would look much different from my fresh start when I left for college. My mind was entirely focused on making the most of my college education and finding a job to start my career. It took many months of refurbishing my resume, submitting job applications, and receiving numerous rejections before I landed the perfect role for myself.

My mom was an excellent support for me during this time. She always saw my potential when I couldn't. She continuously motivated and comforted me in times I was feeling defeated. Every rejection email discouraged me from thinking I would find the job I was looking for. But with every tear, my mom was there, drying them and encouraging me to keep going. She always said, "This is the only time in your life where you have nothing to do but work on yourself."

I was applying for jobs I wasn't exceptionally qualified for, so I got numerous rejections, too many to count. I even worked with a recruiter, and it was apparent that I needed to refine my skillset further as I was not ready to compromise on the type of work I wanted to do.

I started taking business analysis training courses while I continued my job search. This subject was of great interest to me; I liked being on the business side of technology because communication was my strength. My goals were changing, and I worried less about boys and more about feeling good. While job searching, I continued to pour immense energy into my health by working out, eating healthy, and making time for things that were important to me. I was in a good place mentally, so it allowed me the freedom to prioritize other tasks. Taking the business analysis course and succeeding at it revealed another side of me. If I believed in myself and put the work in, I now knew I was capable of anything. This course was fun, and I was good at it. I understood the flow of technology and could reiterate it in layman's terms to clients. This was my forte. For example, say a company is working on building a new mobile application. My job as a business analyst would be to gather requirements on all the functions of the application, detail and document it, get approvals from business clients and then work to test and ensure that the application is functioning accordingly. That's a high-level summary of the job I was looking for.

After a few months of continual searching, my mom came running into my room and said, "I have found a position that I think you might be perfect for."

This was it. I could feel it. The moment I applied for this job, I knew it would be life-changing. My days of hard work on acquiring a new skill would finally pay off. I got the job. I would be a business analyst for a highly reputable company, and my parents were so proud.

Looking back, I can't even imagine how different my life would've looked if I had different parents. In Indian culture, it was preferred that girls be married by a certain age. My parents had asked me about getting an arranged marriage soon after I finished college. It was just the natural next step in life. They were raised with the mindset that at my age, it was time to settle down and find a husband. They didn't force me because I was always my own person, but they had many conversations with me about finding a husband. They were even willing to help me look. But I knew that this was not the path meant for me. And deep down, they knew it too. I stood my ground, asserting my independence. And they supported me fully. My parents then went back to pouring all of their energy into encouraging me to build my career and my life.

I didn't know many people in Chicago, and my new job was in the suburbs. Not the ideal situation, but I knew I was only a car ride or train stop away from the city. I found comfort in this. My parents and I started apartment hunting, deciding that it made the most sense for me to live close to work, so I wasn't spending hours commuting.

My first day of work as a business analyst was exciting. I had my first real big girl job! I was financially independent. I had my own car and apartment. This was the freedom I was searching for. My job was challenging because I had never worked in this field before, so everything I learned was new. I grasped it quickly, and I was good at what I did. My new coworkers were warm and friendly. They were also twenty to thirty years older than me. While I had hoped to meet some people my own age at work, I soon realized that I enjoyed working with people older than me. I was learning a lot from them—both from a work and life perspective.

One of my best friends in the office was much older than me, with sons my age. This relationship became one I would never forget. It only makes sense that colleagues become your work family because you spend more time at work than at home. I was grateful for these connections because I was starting to hate returning to my apartment. It got lonely very fast. I was so used to having my parents and dog or roommates with me all the time, and it was a rude awakening to accept that the transition into being alone wouldn't be easy.

I didn't start to get close to Pixel, my family's dog, until after college. I noticed how attached I was to him when he wasn't around. I would FaceTime my parents and siblings all the time, and even though my brother lived in the city, it seemed so far away. Sunny had been out of the house since he left for college at eighteen. He always knew what he wanted: to be in computer science. He excelled at it and was working for start-up companies. He was doing his own thing.

My apartment complex in the suburbs was filled with families, and it was hard to make friends, let alone find a boyfriend. One day, someone from my high school reached out to me on Facebook. Let's call him Charlie for privacy purposes. I mentioned previously that I had gone through a "glow-up" when I started taking better care of my health, and some of the jocks from my former high school were starting to take interest. Charlie was one of them, and he lived very close to me. He began messaging me, and it wasn't anything but a simple, "Hi, would you want to hang out sometime?"

Charlie made it clear that he was eager to hang out as he only lived fifteen minutes away from me. I hadn't spoken to him much in high school because I was not in the popular crowd. He was a football player and spent his time in a completely different social circle than I did, so our paths rarely ever crossed. I remember him fitting the exact stereotype of a jock back then. At this time in my life, I was excited to hang out with him because I wanted the company. I had no idea what this hanging out would entail, but I was looking forward to the idea of having a friend and perhaps something more.

I specifically remember our first interaction because he couldn't find my apartment. My building was nestled in the back, among many others in the complex. I had to run outside and meet him at a spot he parked four buildings over. I remember giving him a hard time for not following my exact directions. I also vividly remember the gray suit he had on. I thought, *Wow, I love it when a man is dressed in business attire.*

That first hangout was memorable because we sat on my couch and talked all night. There was so much chemistry, and I felt hopeful that this connection would turn into something beautiful. The next day at work, I got another text from him asking if he could see me again the next day. I remember getting butterflies because he was so charming in how he spoke to me. I tend to get attached to people reasonably quickly; sometimes, this was problematic, but in this instance, it was clear he was also catching feelings.

The idea of being alone in that apartment without any friends nearby and with nothing to do was disheartening. This motivated me even more, to hang out with Charlie. We had witty banter and lots of laughter during our interactions. We loved going to restaurants and movies and sometimes just wandered around the city. Soon, it was clear that we couldn't get enough of each other. In just a month, he was practically living at my place. It wasn't official, but he would spend most of the week with me and would rarely ever go back to his apartment.

After a couple of months, it made the most sense for us to officially move in together. The opportunity to have a real relationship with Charlie while hiding this thrilling time of our lives from my parents was bittersweet because I was too scared to tell my parents about him. I never talked about my relationships with my parents or family. It was the most awkward topic of all. So, I just hid the fact that I even had a boyfriend in the first place. Charlie would some-times ask me if we could hang out with my parents, but I would always make an excuse and deflect the conversation. I met his parents, however, and they would visit and hang out with us often. I loved his whole family. There was some familiarity with them, and I was great with parents.

Almost a year into our relationship, I could sense the patterns and signs of codependency returning. We would be with each other most of the time, and I didn't make time for my friends. My friends from college had either moved away or didn't live nearby, and I didn't know how to make new friends living in the suburbs. Everyone around me was older with kids, so Charlie was the only one I had. He didn't have many friends around here either, so we spent all our spare time with each other. And living together made it even harder to find time apart. It was starting to feel a little like it did with Jeremy. It was not a feeling I liked, but it was easier to hang out with Charlie than to leave my apartment and go into the city to hang out with friends. And, because I had Charlie in my life, I didn't think making new friends was important. It was all I knew, and I figured it was healthy and all okay.

There were many good parts of our relationship, and we got along well for the most part. We liked watching movies and playing tennis together. We didn't argue much and enjoyed each other's company. But the feeling of living in suburbia was getting old. I wanted to live in the city and experience new things, and I felt like I was losing myself in Charlie. My whole world revolved around him, and I gave him all my energy. I know now that this was extremely unhealthy, but I didn't think it was a problem back then. So,

I convinced Charlie that we should move into the city. We started apartment hunting and found the perfect little studio in Lakeview.

Charlie wasn't making much money, so I was bringing in most of our income. This was another part of our codependency that I hated. *We weren't married, so why am I the only one supporting our lifestyle?* These thoughts were all internal because I was extremely nervous about bringing this up to him for fear that he might leave me if I made him feel like less of a man. The insecure part of me always thought that if I gave all of myself to him, he would never leave me. My outlook on a healthy relationship was very skewed.

I cooked for Charlie, bought all our groceries, and paid our rent and utilities. I also supported him emotionally. I think a part of me felt responsible for doing all of these things because I felt guilty for not introducing him to my parents. I knew that this was important to Charlie, but I had no plans of making that intro. I think part of the reason was that, deep in my heart, I knew that he might not be suitable for me. My mindset was that I'd only take home the man I knew for certain I was going to marry. My parents wanted me to marry an Indian man because it would be easier culturally. I couldn't take multiple men home. Dating should've been acceptable, and I am sure it could have been. I just didn't want to take various men home. If they were going to be of a different race, I would only take home the one I planned to marry.

Charlie wasn't showing me any signs that he would be the one. I didn't feel like he was committed to helping us build toward the future. Even though this was true, the moments I spent with him on our couch, just talking or playing Mario Kart or watching a movie, were some of my favorite times. I would miss him when I was at work. I am not sure how love can have such opposing sides. Sometimes, I couldn't stand him, and other times I'd find solitude in him.

As the days went on, I could sense Charlie was acting differently. When I first met him, he was career oriented. He was ambitious and driven. Now, I saw him getting comfortable and not trying as hard. This made me nervous, so I changed my behavior around him. There was much tension between us. Unlike my last relationship, I was very vocal in this one. I would point out behaviors in him that I didn't like. He was messy and would leave his things around the apartment. I was also messy at times, and it was frustrating that he added to it.

In mid-fall, about two years into our relationship, I got a well-deserved promotion, and Charlie lost his job. This was a turning point in our relationship. I hated that he was always home in an apartment I was paying for. We had never addressed this topic, and I knew it was finally time to have a conversation with him about our finances. I was so worried that it would end us that I kept prolonging it. I suppressed all my emotions, knowing this was wrong and that I wasn't being true to myself.

There was also another layer of tension because I still hadn't told my parents about Charlie yet. I also didn't talk with my friends about the issues I was having with Charlie because I didn't want them to look at him in a different light. I was fighting an internal battle, and I was struggling. Instead of addressing these issues and conflicting emotions,

I kept going on with life—extremely unhappy. I encouraged Charlie to find a job, but he just had a side hustle as a massage therapist. This profession concerned me because I was not fond of him making house visits to massage other people. But I thought, *Well, at least he is making some money doing this.*

I was making enough money to support both of us, allowing Charlie to figure out what he wanted out of life. Even though I had a great career, I knew this current job wasn't a passion of mine. But I still worked hard and gave my all at work. I got another promotion, and I was incredibly proud of myself. I looked forward to leaving the apartment and going to work simply to avoid spending copious amounts of time with Charlie. We were together all the time when I was home, and it was getting to be too smothering.

Around this time, I returned to using food as a coping mechanism as I had done in the past. I was giving Charlie so much of my energy that I wasn't taking care of my needs. I stopped working out. I started eating more, and I found comfort in that. I loved to cook, so I would use that as an excuse to spend time in the kitchen while he would work on fixing old watches. Don't get me wrong; there were beautiful moments nestled in with all the negative feelings. That's why I stayed in the relationship. I pushed all the negative feelings aside and figured that they would pass—this situation of him not working and being around all the time would change. I convinced myself that the discomfort I was feeling was temporary.

I could sense that Charlie was unhappy in our relationship. There were many signs right in front of me that I ignored. One red flag was when he boldly told me I was gaining weight. He didn't sugarcoat it. I knew I was, but how he expressed it to me was extremely hurtful. Coldly, he said, "You've put on a lot of weight; I think you should hit the gym."

I cried about it when he wasn't around to see, but I remember that I didn't make a change. His words didn't motivate me to work out and take better care of myself. In fact, it did quite the opposite. I turned to food even more. When he wasn't home, I would binge eat everything I could find. After every binge session, I started to hate myself more and more. I knew it was unhealthy, but I didn't care.

Three years into our relationship, I decided it was time to move again. At this time, I was working from home two days a week, so I wanted to live closer to downtown and upgrade my apartment. Even though this meant my commute would be longer, I wanted to take on this added stress for a better place. Charlie was not on board with me spending so much on an apartment, but I didn't particularly value his opinion. It's not like he was helping me with any bills. I was the breadwinner of the relationship, and I wanted to move. He was a little upset with this move but knew he had no choice but to comply if he still wanted to be in this relationship and live with me.

The summer of that year in our new place was tough. I still hadn't told my parents about him because I was so unhappy in our relationship. I know what you're thinking; why would you not just get out of the relationship? Even though I was unhappy, I didn't want to lose my best friend. This had started to become a theme of my dating life; I always care too much about the well-being of others to know that I deserve better.

My parents always wanted to come and visit me, but I would always make an excuse because if they came and saw my place, they would see Charlie's things everywhere. I came up with so many lies to keep them from coming. But once in a while, I couldn't stop them. During those times, I made Charlie leave the apartment, and I would somehow manage to hide all his things. My brother and his girlfriend were also only a couple of miles away. I would never invite them over. I always went to their place to see them or out to dinner. I never included Charlie. I knew this was not normal. How could I continue to live this way? This was my first real relationship where I knew I was fucking it up but continued anyway. It didn't feel right; I hated myself and continued the harmful patterns of eating to cope. As I am telling this story, I cannot believe I let this go on for so long.

Then, fall arrived, and things started to take a terrible turn. My parents called me and told me that my grandmother had passed away. My mom was inconsolable; this was her mom, whom she loved dearly. Her world was flipped upside down. My grandmother lived in India, so my family would have to travel over twenty-three hours to return and attend her funeral. My siblings and I did not go because of work and other responsibilities. My dad later told me that my mom cried the entire flight back to India. This was a challenging moment in our family as it was the first grandparent we lost. The hardest thing was not being close by to visit and see family when they live on the other side of the world. I didn't know how to be there for my mom because it was the first death in the family.

I was trying to process the loss myself, which was tough because I was going through so much unhappiness in my own life. I lied to my parents and siblings about being in a relationship and lied to my friends about the difficulties of it all. I always pretended like everything was okay. Because my parents were going to be in India for a while, I was taking care of our family dog, Pixel. He was the best thing to ever happen to me. The unconditional love I got from him was a godsend. He made life better for Charlie and me. Pixel and Charlie started to create a bond, and I loved seeing that.

Charlie stepped up emotionally for me in this time of despair. I saw a change in him, and it made me feel good that he was supportive and kind. I started to witness his growth in his love for me. Pixel was alone at my apartment when I was at work, but Charlie would take care of him. I was concerned for Pixel when Charlie wasn't around because he had separation anxiety, which worried me. So, I decided to buy a Petcube camera to keep an eye on him while working. The Petcube was a video camera that kept a log of Pixel's movements, and I could even talk to him through it if I wanted to.

A couple of weeks into my parents being gone, Charlie started to act suspiciously. He became a little quieter and reserved. I sensed something was wrong, but he wouldn't tell me anything. I just intuitively knew that he was unhappy. But we kept living together and continued with life as usual. One weekend, my little sister was returning home from college, and I decided to bring Pixel and meet her there since no one else was home. I had this gut feeling that I should leave my Petcube on to see Charlie's whereabouts. I hid the camera behind the

TV so he wouldn't see it and went away for the weekend. That weekend, I was constantly checking on him and verifying that he was telling me the truth over text messages about his plans for the weekend. It comforted me knowing that he was telling me the truth, but then Sunday arrived. I had planned to work from home the next day, so I decided to stay in Bloomington with my sister, Divya, on Sunday night.

Charlie said he would be hanging out at the apartment that night after he finished with his massage client. But I soon discovered that he was lying. He texted me after his appointment, said he was back home now, and said good-night. Of course, I checked the video on Petcube and found to my surprise, that he was not home. Anxiety crept through my blood, and I stayed up all night checking the camera. Somehow, I fell asleep around two in the morning, unable to stay awake any longer. The following day, after my daily work call, I rechecked the camera, and he was still not home. I was panicking.

I didn't get a text or phone call from him. My head was filled with negative scenarios of where he'd been, who he was with, and what he was doing. I decided not to say anything to him until he reached out to me. I was franti-cally checking the camera to see when he'd return. Then, around 9:00 a.m., he came back home. I decided to give him a call, and he answered. I asked him what he was doing.

He lied and said, "I just woke up."

For some reason, I didn't want to confront him from two hours away, and I kept hounding him with questions about his morning.

He got extremely irritated and hung up the phone after

he said, "Why are you asking me all these questions? I have to go and take care of some errands." I checked the camera after he hung up the phone and specifically remembered him throwing his phone onto the couch and yelling out loud, "Ugh, annoying bitch."

My heart broke at that moment, and I knew I had to confront him when I got home. After a few hours, I returned to my apartment and did just that. I started yelling at him and saying I had proof of his lies. I demanded answers as to where he was.

He channeled his anger in that moment towards me. He started yelling at me about spying on him and how I didn't trust him. I could not believe he was flipping this all around on me, and he made it sound so convincing. I knew that spying on him was not right, but I could intuitively sense that he was being untruthful.

After he calmed down, he told me that he was gambling. He was at the casino all night and was trying to win money. This was a shocking and unanticipated discovery because I had no idea he even liked to gamble. Sometimes, when we were on road trips, he would buy lottery tickets or scratch-offs but frequenting the casino was news to me. He showed me his parking ticket and his winnings, and I just had a sigh of relief. I had thought the worst of him. I thought he was cheating on me, and this discovery was alleviating to hear. Yes, it was terrible that he had a gambling problem, but this was much better than the alternative scenarios in my head. I forgave him for lying because I understood it. He was feeling low because he wasn't making much money, and I supported him. I could understand this perspective. We talked about it and were able to get past it.

We went home for Thanksgiving. Charlie and I are both from the same hometown, so we went to our respective childhood homes for the holiday. One of our friends was having a party over the weekend, so we both went. Afterward, we went to the bars and had a great time catching up with old friends from high school. He dropped me off at my parents' house that night, and I went to bed.

The next day, my friend called me and said to come over because she wanted to talk. I could hear in her voice that she was nervous. I hadn't thought anything of it, but I was shocked to hear what she had to say that following day. She told me that after Charlie dropped me off, he called her. It was 2:00 a.m., and he wanted to come to her place to see her and smoke. To this day, I am unsure as to why she said yes. It was odd that my boyfriend was calling her to hang out without me. But alas, she invited him over to her house. While they were hanging out, he tried to kiss her. She resisted and told him to leave immediately. When she spoke these words, my mind went numb, and I could feel anger creeping through my whole body. After everything I had done for him and the excuses I made for his lack of effort, this is what he does to me? I had never experienced this amount of rage, hurt, and sadness in my entire life.

I didn't call him or text him that day. I wanted an explanation and knew I wouldn't get that unless I spoke to him in person. The next day, I went to our apartment in Chicago and started packing all his things. This was it. I was done. There is no way I would tolerate this kind of disrespect. By the time he arrived back at our apartment, I had all his things packed in boxes in the corner of the apartment. As soon as he walked in, he knew it was over. I asked him to explain himself, and he couldn't and didn't. He simply started moving the boxes into his car. He said he was moving back to his parents while he figured out what he would do next. That day, I lost a friend and a boyfriend. I was angry with my girlfriend for allowing him to come over, and I was even more upset with Charlie for his unfaithful behavior.

The few days after he moved out of my apartment were tough; I cried all the time. I was lonely and lost. I missed his presence. I missed how he kissed me goodnight and the times he would make me coffee in the morning. It was the little things.

After the initial shock of it all, I started to come back to myself. At least I had Pixel, which made living alone much more manageable. I decided to keep Pixel at my place for a bit longer and started building back my life.

I got back to the gym and started eating healthier once again. Even though these were good behavioral patterns, I still felt this aching emptiness. I tried to stay busy, but I didn't have many friends with whom I felt comfortable. It was a slow process, but each day it felt more manageable to continue moving forward and reconnect with myself.

My best friend from college, Laura, came and visited me during this time. We had the best weekend full of music, going to restaurants, and catching up. Laura was always there for me without judgment. She accepted my faults in loving Charlie and always gave me her honest thoughts but would never judge me for settling for him. I am not sure what I would have done without her support. I was so grateful to have someone like her in my life to lean on. She became my lifeline.

After a couple of months, Charlie reached out to me again. He said he was moving back to the city and living with one of his friends from high school. This excited me that he would be so close again because I was lonely while he was gone. One night after he moved back, he texted me to hang out. I reluctantly said yes. I missed him and didn't see how catching up would be that damaging. When we saw each other after these few weeks of separation, it felt like a flood of emotions rushing back into my soul. I didn't think all the feelings would resurface as quickly as they did. I guess I wasn't over the relationship. How could I be? We invested three years into it, and it wouldn't just disappear that fast. I had been on dating apps when we separated and enjoyed getting to know other men, but I truly missed Charlie.

We started hanging out again consistently, which was better because, this time, we were not living together. It seemed like the perfect balance of space and quality time. I discovered that I needed some space to ground myself in the relationship. Things seemed to be going much smoother. There were, of course, times when I thought we would not be getting back together again, and this was just a fling—which is odd, considering we had been together three years already. There was no pressure, rules, ties, or commitment. I felt insecure about what we were doing, but I was unwilling to stop because I genuinely cared so much about Charlie. We eventually decided to get back together because the in-between was weird for us. We both realized we wanted each other in our lives. We started hanging out with his family again. I decided that this time around, I was going to tell my parents.

One weekend, I went home, and before returning to my apartment, I mustered up the courage to finally tell my parents I had a boyfriend. Charlie and I had been solid for a while, and I thought it was only right to let them know who I had been spending all my time with. The conversation did not go well. My parents, specifically my mom, made it very clear that he would not be accepted into the family. There were many reasons why she disapproved. We all know by now that they wanted me to be with a South Asian man, and this was when my mom brought up arranged marriage to me again. She reminded me that I could very easily find a good boy. I refused. I didn't want to marry someone by looking at their biodata; that's not romantic. Biodata is a sheet of paper that tells you all about a potential partner. This included their picture, their profession, their parents' backgrounds, their sibling(s) names, and their favorite hobbies. This conversation always sparked an argument, and I didn't have much tolerance for it.

This was one of the reasons why I was so reluctant to introduce Charlie to my family. Another reason was that he did not have a steady job or career. And the third reason was that my mom could see I was unhappy. I had told her about the relationship's longevity, and she told me she knew me inside and out and that something was wrong. She suspected I was with someone all along, but she didn't say anything to me. This conversation ended in a heated argument. I stormed out of my house and didn't speak to them for a few days. I needed that time to let go of the anger I had inside of me for them not accepting my relationship.

My new biggest problem with Charlie was that my family was not accepting him, which built up considerable resentment. Not only did he bring it up in every argument we had, but I could see in his eyes that he was losing faith in the relationship. I knew then that this could never work because how could it? Family is a big part of my life; lying to them over the last few years was the hardest thing I had ever done. I lived a double life growing up as a teen, and I was now doing it again as an adult.

There were also many qualities in Charlie that I disapproved of. His lack of work ethic, his unwillingness to figure out what he wanted to do in life, and his way of thinking didn't align with mine. I was growing tired of maintaining this relationship. Somehow, we still couldn't let each other go. We were just prolonging the inevitable.

One night we got into a huge fight, and Charlie confessed something to me. He told me that he had been cheating on me throughout our whole relationship. I froze. "What do you mean by our whole relationship?" I asked him.

He said he meant right from the start in our very first year that he had been cheating. As if defending his actions, he said, "In my mind, we weren't even officially together until you told your parents, and you hadn't."

There was once a time when I would listen to Charlie's concerns when he brought up my parents. He would often use them as an excuse in arguments for his behavior. I used to believe that he was right, and I would justify his actions. But this time, I saw him for what he truly was: a liar.

My worst fears had come true. The man I had loved and cared for over all of these years had been playing me the entire time. I had been faithful and committed—giving so much of my time and energy to him, even when I had feelings of doubt. And meanwhile, Charlie had been fooling around with other girls behind my back while he completely leached off me financially. I was livid.

He didn't need to say anymore. We were done. He packed his bag and left for good.

Baby Deepti (1991)

Up to mischief as a two-year old

Helping amma in the kitchen

Clearly, I was always into spirituality

On my way to stir up some trouble

Those pigtails lived on until 7th grade

I knew how to smize before it was a thing

Yeah, mom - I know how to babysit

Should my brother bring
those jeans back?

The Three Musketeers:
Me with my brother, Sunny, and sister, Divya

Sunny turns eight

Look at all my cousins

I like school only when
I can wear hats

No one loves you
like your amma

Why didn't I get to be the letter "D"?

Monkeying around

I have so much love for Sunny

Uh oh I forgot all my dance moves

First Time in Chicago (2001)

Mom—why are you making me pose with the principal? (2000)

Views for days (Smoky Mountains 2003)

Surprised I didn't break anything else

Music lessons (2005)

Fresh set of wheels

Middle school isn't
for the weak

My parents (circa 2009)

Eiffel Tower Selfie (2014)

College Bestie, Lo

Louvre Museum (2014)

First day of work (2014)

The takeover of Europe
(Paris 2014)

The Narrows, Zion
National Park

It's always Sunny with Hina (Sunny's Wedding 2017)

Derek becomes my
therapist (2021)

29th Birthday (Singapore 2020)

This is 30

Colorado views (2020)

Bachelorette girls (Love is Blind 2021)

Netflix wedding day

My girls (Caitlin & Dani 2021)

Kyle gets deep
(@ttolbphotog 2022)

Art has no limits nor does love
(@joshbeatonphoto)

Ride or die (Caitlin 2022)

BUILDING BACK CONFIDENCE

"The future belongs to those who
believe in the beauty of their dreams."
– ELEANOR ROOSEVELT

Charlie was out of the picture now but wasn't out
of mind.

I began reflecting on what our time had
looked like together over the past six years. I felt his
absence but needed to sit with the loneliness to realize its
power.

Loneliness is inevitable in life and certainly isn't a
comfortable feeling to experience. On top of that, I felt as if
I wasn't good enough and that I would never find someone
to love me. I was afraid of feeling lonely forever.

Looking back, I realize I didn't even know who I was
anymore when I was with Charlie. Why had I chosen to
stay in a relationship for so long that was no longer serving
me? Why was I so afraid to step out on my own? When you

take off the rose-colored glasses, you see the situation for what it is.

I now see my experience with Charlie as a lesson I had to go through to understand myself better. To be honest, I'm almost thankful that he cheated on me. It was the one action that was so bad that there would be no excuse for it. Every other wrongdoing of Charlie I had forgiven, but this one truly showed me that he was not the man for me. The universe forced me to move on. And I did just that.

It took me a couple of months to realize how much I loved my own company. Unlike before, when I would feel lonely when by myself, I was now seeing how peaceful it was to come back home from work, focus on myself, and not think about someone else. I found comfort and happiness in the little things I loved doing that I had let go of when Charlie was around. I could now work out whenever I wanted to, watch whatever TV show I wanted, and talk to whomever I wanted to. This feeling was liberating.

In the weeks following the breakup, I returned to dating apps to see what was out there. I tend to jump on dating as soon as one relationship ends. I wasn't ready to go on any physical dates quite yet, although I met some potential candidates. I just wanted to find peace in knowing that men were interested in me. I recognize now that this was not healthy. It was a form of seeking attention and turning to external validation instead of looking inward. My battles of insecurity over the years meant I tended to find my worth through others' eyes. As much as I had made a lot of progress in this area, I still had a lot more learning to do.

That is what the next two years of my life would entail—

growth. I realized I had many unhealed trauma and self-worth issues that I needed to work on. I just had to figure out a way to better myself and step into a version of me that I knew existed deep down. Sensing that I wasn't yet in a good headspace to date anyone, I logged off the dating apps to work on myself.

I started to implement changes in my thinking and mindset. How could someone else notice all the good in me if I didn't see it in myself? As the days unfolded, I started to put my thoughts into action. I began to show up for myself and set goals. The first thing I did was change my daily habits. Instead of waking up an hour before work, I would wake up two hours before work and start my day with a vigorous workout. It was hard to implement this at first.

I would make excuses to hit that snooze button until it was too late to work out. And, when I got home, I would make excuses again. I would tell myself, *Oh, work was too hard today, and it's okay not to work out in the evening because of it.* But I didn't let my excuses stop me. Sure, I lacked motivation on some days. But on other days, I would wake up before my alarm and feel amazing after a workout. I knew that consistency was the key to success and so I gave myself grace and removed the pressure of having to get it right every day.

At first, I was just focused on cardio workouts, and my body didn't change. My stamina had improved, but I didn't see any weight loss. This made me regress a little. I would teeter back and forth between committing to be better or giving up. And then I met Tony.

Oh, you thought Tony was another love interest, huh? Nope. Tony was a fitness instructor, and I connected with him virtually. He curated a ninety-day program for me based on my unique needs, and I decided to commit to it. There was a workout plan for every single day. This was perfect because I didn't have to think about it; I just had to act. The plan was already structured for me, and I could choose the goals I wanted to set. I realized the workouts I had been doing previously were ineffective because there was no structure. I needed a professional to help me through this process because I honestly had no idea what I was doing. The workouts I had been doing were not giving me results, and cardio alone was just not cutting it.

I started researching how to lose weight properly. In the past, I had turned to bad habits. I was bulimic, sometimes anorexic. I use the words bulimia and anorexia because I recognize now that these are the categories my actions fall under. I didn't think I had a disorder at the time because I was not acting on it daily. My bulimia was triggered only on the days that I would binge eat my emotions. My anorexia was triggered only when I couldn't cope with my weight gain, and so I would stop eating altogether. My old mindset was that if I just didn't eat, then I would lose weight. This was the unhealthiest way of thinking because, after a few days of this behavior, I would feel low from my lack of nourishment. This low would soon make me want to binge eat because I was severely lacking nutrients. When you stop eating for a few days, your body starts to go into starvation mode. The next time you eat, its initial reaction is to store everything as fat because it's unaware of when you might eat next. On the opposing side, if you constantly give your body the right foods and vitamins, it starts to understand consistency and adheres to your behaviors and thought patterns.

I see now just how disordered my relationship with food really was. These were the old patterns I was trying to break, and having a dedicated program to follow helped me focus my energy in the right place. I had set my goals and intentions, and it was time to put it all into action. I didn't judge myself if I missed a workout here and there. I didn't punish myself if I overate one day. Through this process, I realized that change takes time, and a lifestyle change takes conscious and consistent effort. There were still many days that I would come home and binge. On those days, I went to sleep upset with myself. But the next day, I woke up and started over. It constantly ebbed and flowed. I tried to love myself in the mirror no matter where I was on this journey. Some of the positive affirmations I spoke to myself were things like: "I am worthy. I am beautiful. I do not chase; I attract. I am capable." Don't get me wrong; there were many days that I still felt gross in my own skin. But I knew that speaking negatively to myself would not be part of a lasting solution. This was my journey and my one precious life, and I wanted to make it count.

As you've likely observed from my journey thus far, anytime I've gone through hardship, I've always built myself back up by focusing on healthy habits and routines. Other women often ask me what apps and tools I use to help me feel my best, so I thought I'd share a list of some habits that have completely changed my life.

HABITS AND ROUTINES THAT HELPED ME BUILD
BACK MY CONFIDENCE

Meditation: I learned that sitting quietly with myself and focusing on my breath was a great way to calm my nerves and help me feel present. My favorite app to use is called *Waking Up* by Sam Harris.

Yoga: Yoga is about finding balance. Sometimes life throws us a curve ball, and it feels like we're just going to keep getting hit. That's when we need to take a step back, take care of ourselves, and take time to find a new balance. Yoga can help with that. It strengthens muscles, relieves stress, and calms the body and mind. The movements of yoga help release blocked energy and leave me feeling at peace.

Affirmations: "I am enough."

"I accept myself just the way I am."

"I focus on action to create the life I want."

"I am successful."

"I am confident."

"I am getting better and better every day."

"I do not chase; I attract."

"All that I need is within me."

We all deserve to hear these words but shouldn't count on them only coming from others. We must believe these words for ourselves and repeat them daily. Affirmations can look and feel different for everybody; the key is to pick phrases that align with your life journey and where you want to be. There is power in words, especially the ones you speak to yourself. I recommend taking a few minutes in the mirror every morning to repeat your chosen affirmations and remind yourself of your worth.

Exercise: Walking, lifting weights, workout classes, and playing tennis are a few of my favorite ways to move my body. Enjoyable exercise looks different for everyone. I think it's important to find types of exercise that don't feel like punishment to you but are actually something you enjoy. Movement of all forms is valuable. I also recommend speaking with a fitness professional if you want help getting set up with a customized plan.

Journaling: Throughout the trajectory of my childhood and adulthood, I have found journaling to be therapeutic. I could talk to myself through my journaling even when I couldn't speak to anyone else about my internal battles. When I wrote out my thoughts, I would surprise myself. *Wow, is this really how I feel about the situation?* There is strength in taking time to reflect and discovering all of the emotions you might be harboring inside.

In the winter of 2019, I was excited to see results after months of discipline, especially just in time to go to India for my cousin's wedding. Even though I was not yet where I wanted to be, I was heading in the right direction and could see the progress, which was highly motivating and exciting. I was ready to break from normalcy and see my family in India again. After my breakup with Charlie, I tended to my relationships with my family and spent lots more time with my brother and sister-in-law, Hina. I was eager to go to India and celebrate my cousin and his soon-to-be wife. I focused even more on my exercise regimen because I wanted to look and feel good at the wedding. It was something I was looking forward to.

My extended family in India was never shy about calling out physical appearance. In the past, they had not hesitated to point out the obvious fact that I had gained weight, and this used to trigger me. For this reason, I was a little nervous about going back. I had made so much progress and didn't want to experience a setback. I realized, however, that I felt different about myself this time. Even though I was still overweight, I was happy with where I was and the direction I was going. I was finally starting to take care of myself the *right* way.

Indian weddings are extravagant, and the clothes need to match that vibe. Usually, I dreaded this part of the wedding because I never felt comfortable around my fit cousins, who put much effort into taking care of their physical appearance. I was happy to see that, for the first time, I didn't cringe at the thought of getting my measurements taken so that my Indian outfits would fit me. My aunts and uncles noticed the change in my body. They even congratulated me and asked me what I was doing differently. This made me feel elated. Not only did they notice the change in me, but they were looking for advice on how to do it themselves. I realized that taking better care of myself motivated those around me to do the same.

During my two weeks in India, I did not take a break from exercise. By this time, I had started to feel so much better about myself, and I didn't want to lose the regimen that I had worked hard to build, so I found ways to keep up my routine in India. It was convenient that my uncle had a treadmill, and I brought my resistance bands to India. I would do cardio and then turn on a strength training workout from Tony, my virtual fitness guru. I was beginning to see that working out offered many more benefits than just being fit; it also provided me with incredible mental clarity and feel-good emotions. Even if I wasn't at my goal size yet, working out made me feel better about where I was in my current size.

After the wedding, my parents surprised me with a trip to Singapore for my birthday. I was so delighted because traveling was something I was passionate about. I loved new experiences. I enjoyed immersing myself in different cultures and seeing new architecture.

The night before we were meant to leave for Singapore, the news was blowing up about a virus impacting the east. It was none other than the Coronavirus. At the moment, I was unaware of the severity of the situation, and I thought, *Oh, this definitely doesn't impact me.* I didn't know this could affect our trip. I was wrong. My parents were worried about traveling to Singapore. My dad decided to cancel the trip. I remember feeling incredibly disappointed because I was looking forward to celebrating my twenty-ninth birthday by exploring a new country. Even though I understood the risks, my dad could see the disappointment on my face.

The next morning when I woke, he told me, "We changed our minds; we'll take lots of precautions, but we will go."

Who can say they've blown out twenty-nine candles in Singapore during a pandemic? And here I was, with my family no less. This was one of the best trips ever. We explored all the iconic Singapore attractions. Even the airport was stunning, with its beautiful gardens full of red and yellow flowers. Gorgeous plants surrounded a beautiful waterfall that fell from what seemed like the sky. It's so stunning that most people take pictures of the airport's unique beauty. We went to the botanical gardens and Gardens of the Bay and ate the most delectable food. On the night of my birthday, we ate on the roof of Marina Bay Sands: a three-tower hotel with breathtaking views. It was the trip of a lifetime and a birthday I will never forget. What I didn't see coming was the mess that would be waiting for me when I got back to the States.

Things felt normal for a few weeks when we returned to Chicago after the India and Singapore trips. Then, one day at work, after my morning meeting ended, I walked back to my desk and saw my coworkers frantically packing and shuffling through their things. I didn't know what was happening, but something was clearly wrong. I walked over to my desk and found a note that told us to pack our belongings, and to get out of the office, immediately. I remember walking to my car and thinking, *Okay, this isn't bad at all. I get to go home.* I didn't realize I would never step foot in that office again.

It was COVID that left everyone in such a frantic state. The country declared a state of emergency, and our CEO announced that we would be working remotely until further notice. I went back to my apartment and called my family. They were in the same position as I was and were also told to go home. I didn't understand the severity of the situation and thought we'd be back within the week. There was no way work wouldn't have us come back into the office the following week. Boy, was I wrong.

A couple of weeks passed, and I was still working from my apartment. I realized it was too risky to even hang out with any friends, so I went back home to my parents' place for a little while, waiting for everything to blow over. Since my sister and dog were there, I would have company. That's exactly what I needed because working from home, living alone, and not being able to see anyone was taking a significant toll on my mental health. I was even too scared to go to the gym or grocery store.

Home was comfortable, loving, and warm. My parents took good care of me; I got home-cooked meals, and they even had a gym in the basement! I was excited to continue with my fitness routine. Not to mention, I was surrounded by support and love.

After being at home for two months, my lease ended at the Chicago apartment. It became clear that we were not returning to the office anytime soon, so I decided to give up my apartment and not sign my lease for the following year. I moved all my belongings into storage and emptied my apartment. It felt a little sad leaving because I had a lot of beautiful memories with Charlie there. But Charlie was not in my life anymore, and I had moved on in so many positive ways. It was time to completely let go and move to the next phase of life.

After a few months, the challenges of living at home became apparent. The fear of being stuck there forever always crept into my mind. It brought me back to my old unhealthy habits when I lived at home in my teen years. I knew I had to change my mindset and release those old emotions of feeling trapped. I was a different person now, more mature and more emotionally stable. I liked who I was and was committed to maintaining this new healthy relationship I had cultivated with myself.

One day during the end of that spring in 2020, my best friend, Derek, sent me a posting for a dating show. It came out of nowhere, but he was living in LA at the time and came across the call for Chicago singles. He immediately thought of me. Derek knew my dating history and always reminded me that I deserved better. He saw my potential and told me that I was a catch. He also knew I always wanted to do things differently. And the thought of finding love on a dating show certainly qualified as different.

When I first saw the application, I thought, *Damn, this is an extensive application.* I faintly remembered watching season one of *Love Is Blind* back in February. I loved the concept because it genuinely explores the idea of falling for someone without ever seeing them. This concept was very different from a typical dating reality show, and I was intrigued. All these years, I had struggled with my physical appearance, and now someone could get to know me without seeing me. Maybe it would be a chance to truly meet my match.

Before filling out that application, I never really thought about what I was looking for in a partner. And I sure as hell never vocalized it or wrote it down. After writing down my responses to a few of the questions, I paused. *Why am I even bothering with this detailed questionnaire?* I thought. I decided not to submit an application because, in the back of my mind, I knew my parents would never allow me to go on a television show, especially one about dating. The incomplete application lingered in my mind when I went to bed that night.

When I woke up the next morning, I don't know what came over me, but I decided I needed to finish the application. I took the time to carefully fill out what I was looking for in a relationship—in this case, a marriage. I submitted it without telling anyone except my friend, Derek.

I heard back from the casting agent the next day. The email read: "I'm the Casting Manager for *Love Is Blind*. We are moving you along in the process, and the next step is to fill out a questionnaire for our team. It is LONG (200 questions), but the details and information you give are key to ensuring we have a person in the house who fits what you're looking for!" They also wanted to set up a time to talk on a Zoom call. I was excited but anxious.

Over the next few months, there were follow-up calls and interviews with more in-depth questions about me and the characteristics I was looking for in a life partner. This possibility of being cast for the show was becoming more of a reality, and I decided to tell my family about it. They were terrified. My brother Sunny, and Hina, my sister-in-law, got on a FaceTime call with the rest of our family to determine whether this was something I should keep moving forward with. We took the time to understand its implications and consequences. Ultimately, we decided together that I take the leap.

I couldn't believe that my parents supported my decision to go through this process. They were excited at my potential to meet someone and settle down. My mom always spoke of how she thought I would find a nice Indian man to marry. And I always said to them I would never choose an Indian man. When I say this out loud now, I don't like how it sounds. It sounds like I had something against Indian men. But that's not how I meant it. I think part of my lack of interest in dating an Indian guy was because I wanted to rebel against what my parents wanted for me. Also, I was never around many Indian guys growing up, so I developed my crushes and attraction based on the types of guys with whom I saw and interacted with regularly.

I have not closed myself off from seeing the potential of marrying an Indian man. The main thing is that I want to find someone organically, not from sorting through sheets of paper and looking at the biodata of men with my parents. Getting the opportunity to be part of the *Love Is Blind* experiment might allow me to meet someone whom I genuinely connect with for all of the right reasons.

After a couple of weeks of questionnaires and interviews, I got an exciting email. It read: "Hello and happy Friday! I just want to update you that you will receive our contract later today! At this time, I want to inform you that you are now in a SELECT GROUP of people moving forward. Hooray!"

My family and I took the time to read through this contract carefully. I didn't want to sign my life away. I wanted to ensure this was a good fit. Sunny, Hina and Divya helped me read through every word with my parents before I even thought about signing. This was a big deal. I thought to myself, *How will this impact my career? What would people at work say if they saw me on a dating show? Is it worth doing? Will I even find a person?* There were many doubts about signing. Ultimately, after pondering it for a few days, and with my family's blessing, I signed.

After I signed the contract, there were large gaps in wait

times. The pandemic was getting worse, and the show was pushed further out. Every time I saw an email come through about the show, I got excited. And then, after reading through and learning that the show was being pushed back to a later date again, I was disappointed.

We had to continue living life, and Bloomington was getting old. As a family, we thought about driving to Colorado to stay with Sunny and Hina. There was no chance we would fly because my dad had diabetes; therefore, if he got the Coronavirus, it could be life-threatening. We did not take any chances. At first, he was very reluctant to drive or leave the house. At this point, we were sanitizing every grocery item that we bought. After days of convincing, my parents finally agreed to make the drive as a family.

Colorado was the biggest pandemic blessing, and we enjoyed ourselves so much that we decided to stay there for four months. We were able to go out into nature, hike, and enjoy the outdoors again. The change in scenery was precisely what all of us needed. I loved taking Vino, Sunny's Goldendoodle, on trail runs and being active. I was thriving in Colorado. After a few months of living there, we returned home to Bloomington. After just a week of being back, I was already missing our Colorado adventures. Divya and I were plotting ways to go back.

Then, the perfect opportunity came—Sunny's birthday. We thought it would be an amazing surprise to show up again at his house in Colorado. Hina helped us plan this surprise. She was good at that. She took great joy in making others happy, and Sunny was always first on that list. I admired her ability to bring the family even closer together. So, my sister and I made the fourteen-hour road trip one day to surprise him. Boy, was he surprised! And our time visiting turned into another great adventure. We ended up staying with them for another month.

Sunny and Hina were always also very into fitness. Staying active was a part of our day-to-day regimen. Sunny encouraged me a lot during this time, and we would do workouts together. We also established healthy eating habits. We talked about new ideas and had many intellectual conversations. Sunny didn't like to talk about other people; he saw it as a waste of time. He was always innovative, thinking of new ways to use technology to help ease life. It was an excellent environment to be in. I simply did not want to leave. I've always wanted to live in Denver but was too scared to make the move alone. So, when my brother moved there, I was so grateful to live through him vicariously and make many visits.

We decided to travel to Zion National Park for Sunny's birthday. His friends made the trip from LA and joined us because they also needed a break from their pandemic-ridden lives. Zion was a beautiful place. We loved exploring the trails, and I especially loved the Narrows.

That trip was incredibly bonding for my siblings and me. On one evening, we stayed up all night and just talked about our lives. I spilled all the secrets I'd kept from them over the last few years—from my boyfriends to my partying in college to some of my self-image struggles. My brother and I had had a high-level relationship in the past. I didn't share much of my life with him, so he had no idea what I had been through or had done. The truth is, I never felt comfortable talking about my hardships or relationships with any of my family members. I always had a guard up and felt like I needed to protect myself and my freedom. That night, I told my siblings everything. They were in awe of the unknowns of my life. It all came as a shock to them, but at the same time, they now understood me a little better, bringing us closer together.

I remember my brother praising my strength. He told me that he was proud of me and saw me differently because of all that I had been through. He recognized the effort I was making to become a better me. This meant the world to me because, on some level, I realized I had been trying to make him proud of me my whole life. He was a hard one to crack because Sunny was brilliant and strong-willed. He didn't like drama or sugar-coating things. This was challenging for me because I didn't like tough love. But, to see him become vulnerable that night and understand my emotions was exactly what I needed to feel closer to him. I will remember this road trip for the rest of my life because it was the one where my brother and I finally connected.

The show was still at a standstill when we returned to Bloomington after that trip. The leaves changed colors and dropped to the ground. Slowly, winter crept in, and days got shorter. I still couldn't believe we were in the thick of the pandemic, and the country was in chaos. We were trapped in our homes without access to extended family or friends. I hadn't seen my friends in months. I couldn't risk coming home with the virus and putting my parents in danger. So, my sister and family were my only social life. I browsed dating apps occasionally, but there was no point because it's not like I would even be able to meet them. The thought of FaceTime dates was disheartening. So, I continued the self-love journey. I knew, eventually, the show would get back to me with filming dates. I would wake up each day and check emails, hoping I would have some good news in my inbox. That day did not come that year. Mid-December, my family decided to go back to Colorado to spend the holidays with all of us together. The months were flying by.

My thirtieth birthday was around the corner. I was sad that I wouldn't be able to celebrate with my friends; however, my family made up for all that I was missing out on. They planned the most amazing birthday celebration and rented a beautiful cabin in Breckenridge, nestled in the mountains. It was the perfect getaway. While I was asleep, they woke up at midnight and decorated the entire cabin with thirtieth-year décor. Thirty is a significant birthday; I always envisioned it being in Mexico, partying somewhere beautiful by a beach. But I was extremely grateful and loved that I had a family that cared so much for me. They went above and beyond to ensure I felt loved on this special day. Divya got a hold of all my friends, aunts, uncles, and cousins to compile a video of birthday messages that brought me to tears. It was the perfect day, and I will cherish it forever.

A month after my birthday, we headed back to Bloomington for what seemed like the hundredth time. I was dreading it but knew it was time to head home. The COVID routine continued, and I focused all my energy on work and taking care of myself. When it came time to film, I wanted to look my best. It was amazing to step back and realize that I had lost over seventy pounds over the last three years. All of the small positive changes that I had made in my mindset and habits had compounded, and I was feeling the best I had ever felt.

Then one day, a short while later, I got a phone call. And finally, it was *the* call. After a much-anticipated Zoom meeting, I was told that I would be leaving to film in LA in April 2021. I was ecstatic. I had waited almost a year for this news to come.

Had the show been called to film any sooner, I don't think I would have been emotionally prepared. I realized that the delays in filming had actually served as a blessing for me. I needed the time to heal my traumas from past relationships, build a stronger bond with my family, and grow. Lying in bed the night before my flight to LA, I played the year back in my head. I thought of all the hard work I had put in. All the time I invested in my career. The bonding experiences I had with every single one of my family members. The time I spent with Pixel. The love I developed for health and fitness. The powerful relationship I had built with myself. All of it had contributed to me feeling healthy and whole.

It was time to enter a new chapter of my life.

I didn't know it then, but nothing would be the same again.

IS LOVE BLIND?

"They're beautiful not because
they're fashion queens, they're
beautiful because they know who
they are, and they like themselves."
– NICOLE DIROCCO

Finally, the time arrived.

Getting the opportunity to be a part of *Love Is Blind* was so exciting to me. And the filming came right at a wonderful time in my life when I was feeling in complete alignment with myself. Every day, I poured love and kindness into my body and soul, and the effects of that were noticeable in my mood and physical appearance. There's a different vibrational frequency you operate on when you put this much care into yourself.

The phone call from the producers solidified that I was attracting what I desired: new experiences and the potential to find the love of my life. And it was now time to start seeing it unfold.

Packing for this trip was so enthralling. How do I dress? Do I wear what's comfortable or what's expected? If it were up to me, I would be living in athletic clothes every second, but I knew I had to turn it up a notch. As I was picking out dresses, I felt compelled to accessorize with Indian jewelry. I was starting to see the beauty and richness of my culture, a culture that I had run away from for many years of my life.

Looking back, I can see how much I wanted to fit in. I remember how I tried to change things about myself to be accepted. In this new stage of life, I began to realize that true beauty comes from embracing my uniqueness. Part of that uniqueness is my bicultural identity, and I started enjoying leaning further into embracing my Indian heritage.

My mom was a great support as always, helping me pack for the trip and putting so much time and effort into selecting the perfect jewelry to match my outfits. I really can't take any credit for my fashion sense during the show; it was all her.

As I was trying on bathing suits, many doubts about what looked good crossed my mind. I wondered if other women even thought about these things. There are so many imperfections on my body, and I was only starting to get comfortable with the idea of showing it off. I have stretch marks from losing so much weight, and my brown skin only amplifies the marks. I also have saggy skin in a few areas due to my weight loss. I was trying to suppress my feelings of insecurity regarding my body, but those emotions overflowed my mind. Then, anxiety crept in. I started to question myself and thought, *Could I possibly be the type of girl confident enough to show off my body on television to millions of people? How will I be compared to the other girls? Dare I put myself out there and risk being ridiculed for the rest of my life?* And then, I realized the answer was a clear "yes." I was done living in shame. It was time to get out of this cage and fly, no matter the consequences.

I remember feeling every possible emotion on the flight to LA. I was sad to leave my family, friends, and familiarity, but I was excited about all the new possible beginnings. I was fearful of the outcome, but mostly, I was hopeful that I would find my unique love story—the kind of love hopeless romantics dream of. While pondering these thoughts and listening to Dean Lewis on the airplane, I noticed a young woman beside me writing frantically in a notebook. I thought, *She must be a student trying to get as much work done as possible before this plane lands.* A couple of hours later, I saw the same girl in the bathroom; I looked over at her and politely asked why she was in LA.

She responded, "Oh, I'm just here visiting some friends. You?"

We looked at each other and paused for a moment, and I causally paralleled her response. "Yes, same," I answered.

The airport luggage carousel wait felt like an eternity. I had no idea what my next steps were or who was about to pick me up. As I was people-watching, I could see from across the airport that a man was walking around with a tablet. He was making his way around the carousel, checking in with people, looking at his screen, and moving on to the next person. My stomach dropped, and the nervousness hit me with a gut-wrenching punch. This was it. These women were my competition. I do remember thinking to myself how gorgeous everyone looked.

Like clockwork, the thoughts of uncertainty fluttered through my body. At that moment, I had to converse with myself as I often did to navigate my thoughts in situations like this. I had to remind myself that I could admire people without comparing them to me. I had to retrain my thoughts moment by moment to allow myself some grace. I reminded myself that I, too, was gorgeous and worthy. It was not a competition against each other. If anything, we would all be leaning on each other during this shared experience. We are all just trying to find love and hoping our Prince Charming might be on the other side of this experiment.

Once I gathered my things and my thoughts, we were all led to the arrivals section. I remember looking around at all the women and the copious amounts of luggage we all managed to drag from Chicago and thinking, *Thank goodness I wasn't the only one to overpack.* They broke us into groups and assigned us a van to load into. I was still anxious and only could see some of the girls as we were all spread out around the curb with our things. There were two other girls in my van, and once we settled down for a minute, I looked in front of me and was shocked to see the girl who had been sitting next to me on the plane. We looked at each other and just started dying laughing. I remember she said, "Oh, okay, so you just lied straight to my face, huh?"

I responded, "So did you, woman." This was Natalie.

What are the chances that the same person I was sitting beside on the plane ends up in my van? It was meant to be that way because I recall we had a conversation that day about our responsibilities as Asian women to represent ourselves with grace and authenticity. It may not seem like it matters, but we knew people would watch us later and that ethnicity would be a factor that would be talked about.

Orientation was an out-of-this-world type of experience. I looked around the room and felt the energy of all the women. This was where we would be left entirely to fend for ourselves without outsourcing help from the outside world. We were entering the bubble we would be in for the next three weeks. It didn't seem that long then, but it would be one of the craziest roller-coaster rides I'd ever ridden.

I looked around the room, thinking that all fifteen of these girls would be dating the same men I would. To the outside world, this may seem like a wild concept. Think about it like this—we were all there to find love, and just like a dating app, we were going to swipe through these men, and the only difference was that we couldn't see the men, but we could talk to each other. Oddly, this was comforting to me. We were all going to experience the same thing from totally different perspectives. We were all in this together. My roller-coaster got a few more riders, and we were buckled in to start the ascend.

We got to our hotel rooms, which would be my haven for the next three weeks, I unpacked my suitcase, and to my surprise, inside, I found a little envelope from my mom. She had written me sweet, encouraging messages to read for every day I would be gone. I remember reading every single one of them that first day and coming to tears. It reminded me that she was always thinking of me no matter where I was or what I was doing. I remember feeling her comfort in those moments, and all my anxieties were suppressed. One specific note resonated with me. "Show up authentically as yourself and trust your intuition to lead you when you feel lost." I hope she knows how much her words in those notes meant to me.

The next day, we got ready, and all met in the hotel lobby to go on set for day one of filming. All the girls looked beautiful. While I gravitated mainly toward Danielle, Natalie, Caitlin, and Juhie, I spent time chatting with every single girl and loved each of them uniquely. Juhie was also South Asian, and her family was from Hyderabad. What are the chances that two desi girls ended up in the same situation? I vividly remember thinking, *Wow, this cast is extremely diverse.*

I had this overwhelming confidence when I first got into the pods because I felt like I finally knew my worth. This was a foreign feeling for me because I had struggled with self-esteem issues my whole life. I paused for a moment of gratitude before my first day of dates began and reflected on how far I had come. All of the ups and downs I'd overcome had led me to this moment, and I felt proud knowing that I had persevered.

My first day of dating was fun. I met many interesting men. My number one person was Sal. There was just something about his emotional vulnerability that was charming. He had an amazing voice that I could listen to for hours. After finishing my dates on that first day, my top choices were: Sal, Shayne, and Kyle. What I found most interesting was that I could rank my top choices solely on voice and conversation, not how they looked.

As you can see, Shake was not at the top of my list after the first day. And we'll get into the details of that later. Juhie and Iyanna had friend dates with Shake during the pods, and they were the two that actually made me change my mind about Shake enough to give him a chance. They each had two different perspectives about him on their dates. It was nice to get insight into the other side of his personality that he hadn't demonstrated to me ... yet.

My dates with Kyle were quite memorable and fun. He was easygoing and didn't take himself too seriously. He was constantly burping and farting. This spoke to his silly nature. Those were the dates I enjoyed—the ones filled with goofiness and witty banter paired with deep conversations about life.

As we progressed through the pod dating process, a few people were sent home. We were told they weren't making the connections that they anticipated. Soon enough, the number of people involved in the dating experience dwindled to just ten men and ten women.

This meant the pod dates lasted longer. We spent over two hours with our top four people each day. We would also have night dates with at least three of the men.

We all had diaries with our names on them. At the end of each day, we would rank the men based on preference, and they did the same. And, every morning, we got our diaries back with a schedule attached of times and the location of what pod we'd be in. Sometimes, there would be fun games in the pods. This was to ensure that we could partake in various activities with our person, just like in real life. It simulates the same experience as a real date; we just couldn't see each other.

There were pockets of time where we girls weren't in the pods and instead spent our time in the lounge. Sometimes there were many of us in the lounge at once, and other times there would only be one other girl. This one-on-one time was when the deepest connections were built. To me, this was one of the most memorable parts of pod dating.

Some girls expressed their deepest emotions and life stories. This brought us closer. We would sit in tears, listening to each other's stories of hardship and encouraging one another. We talked about past relationships, the hurts we all went through, the struggles of life circumstances, and childhood trauma. Some were quick to share, but others were more reserved. It was interesting to see how we were all going through the same experience with the show, but it impacted each of us differently. It was comforting to know that no matter how the dates in the pods went, my girlfriends were there to chat with me about it afterward. This show brought me some of the closest friendships I have ever experienced, and I will cherish them forever. I know most of the other girls would agree with me.

People often ask me why I signed up to be on *Love Is Blind*, and my answer is always the same—I wanted to find a unique love story. And a unique story is exactly what I got.

ABHI SHAKES ME

"When someone shows you who you are,
believe them the first time."
– MAYA ANGELOU

The power of authentic connection can be found in the least likely of places. And I was about to find out that one of those places could be within a pod. Let me explain.

When I first met Shake, I dismissed him because something just didn't click for me. I didn't take him seriously. I don't want you to get the wrong idea, I didn't completely write him off, but I didn't rank him high. We had a fun first date, and of course, I was trying to be likable just like everyone else. From the start, you could tell Shake lacked self-awareness, even knowing that what he was asking and saying wasn't appropriate. I was still polite throughout our first date, which was only fifteen minutes long.

He said, "My name is Abhishek, but I go by Shake. My serious relationships have all been blonde. I just remember moving to America and seeing two things for the first time. One was snow, and the other was blondes. And I felt the same way when I saw both." It was clear it was a happy emotion.

I found this to be funny. I thought that maybe he just had a unique personality. You tend to move on when someone tells you they're into blondes, and your type is the same, right? Why would I rank him high when we both have different tastes? We talked about the fact that my two ex-boyfriends were white. I usually go for Caucasian men because I didn't grow up around many Indian guys. This was the reality of the situation. It's not as if I didn't want to; I just didn't have that exposure.

We still got paired together as there were many dating rounds, and we had a second date. On this date, he asked me, "Would it be a problem to lift you on my shoulders?"

I liked witty banter, so I said, "I don't know; are you strong enough to lift me on your shoulders?"

He took great concern with that response. So much so that he asked another guy, Vito, from the show about me. Vito was another cast member who coincidentally went to the same college as me. Because we knew each other, we didn't have a second date.

Shake asked him, "Hey, you went to the same college as Deeps; what does she look like?"

To which Vito responded, "Oh, she had a glow-up. That's all I'll say."

So, right off the bat, he was worried about physical appearance, which is one hundred percent okay. The problem was that we were here for a social experiment to see if you could first fall in love with someone's personality, heart, and energy. If he cared so much about physical appearance, *Love Is Blind* was probably not the dating show for him. I only learned of this conversation months after filming wrapped.

The other guys had such profound questions, and Shake's were shallow from the start. I pursued other guys more than Shake. Somehow, though, we made it to our third date, where we could get into a much deeper conversation since the dates were now extended to an hour-and-a-half. On this date, Shake and I connected on our upbringing and childhood. Culturally, we both had a lot to relate to. He understood the hardships of coming to America at a challenging age, and we both discussed all the ways we had tried to fit in when we arrived. We also agreed that we became whitewashed in the process.

We connected on our love for music, and I was starting to see some mutual interests. The more I talked to him, the more I felt like I extracted these deep emotional thoughts from him. My mindset started to shift. Maybe this is someone I can see a future with. As the days and nights of talking with Shake continued in the pods, I saw this new side to him—potential.

The road to choosing Shake was nothing short of an uphill battle. He was already making other women uncomfortable on their dates with him. Shake made three women cry, which was (obviously) a huge turnoff for me. He was asking if they were "bottle girls" (these are girls that work in clubs), but he said it as if it was degrading. I didn't like that. He also asked other girls if he could carry them on his shoulders, and they found it upsetting. One of the girls didn't feel a connection with him and wanted to end the date early, to which he retaliated, "No one here even likes you; they all think you're so stuck up." Naturally, that's upsetting to hear. I second-guessed ranking him higher.

I went into our next date upset and spoke to Shake about it. I asked, "Why do you think it's okay to talk to women like this?"

This triggered an even deeper conversation between us. He seemed to be able to get vulnerable with me and understand that what he said wasn't okay. He was saying all the right things to me about this situation. He realized that the words he uttered were something he needed to reflect on.

I thought about my own shortcomings for a moment. I was certainly not perfect. I had made mistakes in my life and in turn, learned big lessons from them. At that moment, I felt empathy for Shake. Perhaps he had just made a mistake. I couldn't completely shut him out over it because I understood his perspective. This conversation also led to another deep topic—one about weight loss.

As you know by now, I put in much effort to lose weight, and it took a long time for me to be comfortable talking about it. When I was heavier, I avoided taking pictures and being seen in public; I was ashamed. So, I was extremely nervous to talk to Shake about this experience knowing that he asked so many superficial questions and cared so much about physical appearance. But when we had the conversation, I was pleasantly surprised by his response. He opened up to me about his childhood similarities, further bonding our connection.

I started the conversation and asked, "Did I ever tell you I lost a ton of weight?" knowing full well that I hadn't yet. I followed that up by telling him I had lost close to eighty pounds.

His response was completely unexpected. He said, "Wow, how am I the one asking girls these superficial kinds of questions, and like, nobody else is? And then, I kind of felt ashamed and embarrassed that I did. And I'm like, wow, this is the experiment where you're not supposed to even think about that stuff. It's just ironic." These reflective moments are what made me understand him more.

He continued. "I was chubby growing up. I think I had many body image issues about myself."

This was another complete shock to me. A good kind of shock. No one understood this experience better than I did. I just quietly listened, letting him share his past.

He elaborated. "Because I was out of shape growing up and always uncomfortable, I would compensate by being with somebody in good shape. I'm looking at it objectively now. And it's probably as a result of this experience."

This gave me hope that he was correcting his errors and had the self-awareness I thought he lacked on our first few dates. I thought, *Maybe Shake has been asking so many inappropriate questions of women because of his own body issues.*

He continued. "Everybody has their demons, and maybe I had more demons in this department than I thought."

That was my ah-ha moment. I felt like I could forgive his previous comments because he was genuinely growing into a better person right in front of me. He was self-reflecting on his actions and willing to change his outlook. It made me so happy that he trusted me enough to be vulnerable with me.

It was a special feeling to be connecting with someone who finally seemed to understand my background, upbringing, insecurities, and worries. Whenever I shared a story, he reciprocated with his own meaningful childhood stories that resonated with me. This idea of a shared past made me feel safe. The pods were an environment filled with intense emotion, and the more time I spent with Shake, the more I started to care for him. I started envisioning what it would be like to meet, touch, and kiss him.

We had a day in the pods where we gave each other gifts which made our date extra special. He was perfect on this date. I made chicken tikka masala with white rice and masala chai in our lounge kitchen, and the production team delivered it to Shake's side of the pod. As I arrived in the pod that day, he had a Milk Bar cake waiting for me because I had mentioned it was my favorite on one of our earlier dates. This was incredibly thoughtful and kind. It showed that he listened to me and cared enough to act on it.

We exchanged the gifts we got each other. He gave me a framed picture of his dog, Bandit. He said, "Look at the note I wrote you on the back."

I could recite those words by memory in the months we were together; they were that impactful to me. It started with, "If you are reading this, it's too late. I've fallen for you." He said he knew his heart would be taken care of and signed it from himself and Bandit. This date was memorable to me and left me with a full heart. It was clear we had a meaningful connection.

On our night dates, we talked about our careers and goals. We discussed how we both wanted to be financially independent. That's how my parents raised me to be. We talked about how many kids he wanted. He told me he wanted more than one kid. I said, "I want as many kids as I can afford."

He liked that because it was practical, which seemed important to him. I had always said I wanted to build an empire with someone, and he had the same goals for his future as I did. He would say things to me like, "I just know we're going to have smart, awesome kids."

Hearing those words from him gave me butterflies. He was just as excited about our future as I was. To me, our vision of the future was aligned, and that made me hopeful.

We talked about the Indian culture and what it meant to us as we had both grown up and changed over our adult lives. One thing I brought up was how in the South Asian culture, women are supposed to touch the man's feet when they get married. I said, "Fuck that. We are equals, and I am not touching your feet."

It was comforting when he said, "I am right there with you."

Our talks like this brought us closer, and we just knew that we were each other's one. I could feel a proposal coming.

Then proposal day came. Although it wasn't clear that it was that day, I could feel it. I recall being extremely nervous walking into the pod. I knew he was just as nervous on the other side. I remember precisely when he started to speak, a wave of calmness came over me. It just felt right. As always on our dates, Shake was good with words and knew how to articulate himself. And he set up the proposal perfectly: "I wanted to say something from the heart here.

When coincidence seems too convenient, I prefer to call that fate. And I've never met someone who seems to understand me the way you do. Our stories are so similar, and they've begun to intertwine already. You make me feel some type of way."

This was a perfect addition because I say that phrase a lot. It was personal to me.

He finished with, "Deepti, will you make me the luckiest man in the world and marry me?"

Of course, I had to respond with a yes. I said, "Abhi, I never thought I would meet someone like you, and I feel like fate has just moved us toward each other. A thousand times, yes!" And just like that, we were engaged.

When I returned to the lounge, I was excited to tell the girls about my engagement. They all saw it coming, and they celebrated and congratulated me. By this time, only Danielle was engaged (to Nick). I could tell most were still nervous about their own outcomes. All I wanted to do was tell my family and friends back home. I was whisked away into solo interviews, and I never saw any of the girls again that day.

I recall waiting for Caitlin to get back to her hotel room. Her room was across the pool on the other side, and we would slide the window open to talk. I was anxiously awaiting her arrival back at the hotel. She had been unsure if Joey would propose that day. I was thrilled for her when she yelled across the resort, pointing to her engagement ring. She said, "I'm engaged!" but followed with a gesture of a house. She then said, "I'm going home." This saddened me, but I realized we were about to walk our own paths.

I was extremely nervous about my reveal with Shake.

Would he like my physical appearance? I questioned it, but I was hoping our talks had meant something. *He was starting to see past superficiality* I told myself.

I, on the other hand, wasn't so concerned with his appearance. But I knew in the back of my mind that it mattered to a certain degree. We needed to be physically compatible, too. All my body image issues resurfaced within me. I had to pause and remind myself that I was beautiful, kind, and intelligent. Self-confidence is not just something that comes naturally to me; it's something I need to work on every day. When I have feelings of self-doubt, the conversation I have with myself following those negative thoughts has to be carefully curated. Rewiring your brain takes time and constant effort.

All of my fears about the reveal were centered around how Shake would respond to me when he saw me. I was curious to see his initial facial reaction, what he would say, and how he would act. At this moment, I didn't even think about the reverse situation of my reaction to him.

Waiting for those doors to open was the most anticipated moment of my life. Seeing his silhouette just waiting on the other side was exciting. I was on a roller-coaster of emotions. I couldn't breathe. I wanted those doors to open and to finally lay eyes on him. When the doors finally opened, his eyes instantly widened in awe. He came running to me, and the first words I heard were, "Holy shit, you're so beautiful." He immediately went in for a kiss.

I loved that it gave me butterflies. For the rest of this moment—including when he grabbed my ass—I blacked out, honestly. I was so overwhelmed that it seemed like my brain had just shut off. I was taking his lead, and all I could think to say was "Hi" a million times over.

He got down on one knee, and as he knelt, he touched my feet. This was a beautiful gesture because, as I mentioned before, the wife typically touches her husband's feet in traditional Indian culture when they get married. For him to do that in a reverse way for me meant a lot. He said, "I'd do it for you." He walked me to his side of the door, and we sat down. We kissed the entire time. My lipstick was smeared all over my face, and I'm sure it was not a pretty look walking back to my side of the doors. I knew I should've bought that smear-proof lipstick.

While I was excited to see Shake again and eagerly awaited our next encounter, I couldn't help but feel some fear. There was chemistry at our reveal, but I didn't feel quite myself for some reason. I cried as soon as I returned to my hotel room following our very hands-on reveal. What just happened? Did that feel right to me? Everything was so uncertain. I know in the moment, I pretended it was appropriate when he grabbed my ass because it seemed he was physically into me. But, as I started playing back and processing that moment in my head, I realized how inappropriate it was for him to have done so. Our family, friends, and work colleagues would all be watching. Our future kids might see that someday and it left me feeling upset.

Some of you may ask why I didn't speak about the inappropriateness of the ass grabbing, and the answer is simple —I didn't want to hurt Shake's image in the public eye. I was cautious about what I would say on camera because I knew its implications. Words are powerful, and I wanted to ensure I tailored them in a way that wasn't harmful. I didn't want to be the reason why anyone would be upset. I genuinely cared about Shake and understood that people could make mistakes without realizing them. I thought, *Well, maybe he couldn't control it.*

There were so many eyes on us at that moment, so I could see how his judgment could have been faulty. But even then, thoughts of doubt crept into my mind, and I couldn't help but feel overwhelmed. I wrote my thoughts, feelings, and anxieties in my journal back in my hotel room that night. Journaling helps me cope with stress because I can articulate my feelings better in writing. My honest thoughts flow onto the paper, and the ideas and perspectives I have within sometimes even surprise me. I don't fully register what I'm feeling in the moment. Instead, my emotions often seem to come out more clearly once the words are scribbled on paper, transferring straight from my soul through the pencil.

I didn't see Shake for three days after that until we were in Mexico. I couldn't even recall what he looked like. Our reveal felt like a blur to me. Did we have a good connection in person? Was he attracted to me? Was I attracted to him? I talked myself out of the doubt and decided that I must at least give this relationship a chance. I firmly believe that everything happens for a greater purpose. There was a reason I was supposed to meet Shake.

Walking into my room with Shake on our first night in Mexico felt odd; it was the first time I saw him after the reveal. Showing up in the same hotel room together felt a lot like the feeling you would get if you were going on vacation with a friend's friend. I thought, *Who is this guy, really*? I realized that I didn't fully know Shake yet and had much to learn about him. I had to learn what his body language was like. I had to observe the patterns of his thoughts. In many ways, I was engaged to a stranger, and this was my chance to truly get to know him.

When we first got to the hotel room, we couldn't keep our hands off each other. We were touching and kissing nonstop, and it felt so natural. He gave me butterflies, and I wanted to spend all day in his arms. I found him attractive, and gauging by the intensity of our physical interaction, I felt like he was feeling the same way about me. We were also compatible on many levels, and knowing that we had first connected on an emotional level just made the physical connection much more electric. I was beginning to feel like I was in a fairy tale. Maybe I had found the one for me.

We decided to go out for a swim. This was the part I had been terrified of—putting on my bathing suit. My stretch marks and loose skin were about to be on full display. Walking out into that pool was a scary moment; his eyes would only be on me. But I calmed myself down and remembered how far I had come in my self-love journey. *He already likes you, Deepti*, I thought; you *don't have to fear being vulnerable with him.*

And then, my worst nightmare came true. I could feel his energy shifting as soon as he saw me getting into the pool. I pretended not to notice. I didn't want to be awkward and for him to know that it affected me. Though, inside, I had an agonizing feeling of rejection. My intuition was kicking in, but I have a good poker face. It took me back to all the times I had felt insecure in the past and brought me to a dark place. At that moment, it felt like all the work I put in to see myself differently went out the door. But I told myself that maybe I had read the situation wrong. I mean, he couldn't keep his hands off me earlier, so perhaps it was just the cameras making him feel uncomfortable.

We spent a bit longer in the pool, making jokes, kissing, and holding each other. Then we dried off, had dinner, and spent the night in our hotel room. We had many intimate moments that night, which of course, made me feel closer to him. I felt hopeful about this experience and my relationship moving forward with Shake.

The following day, we woke up and sat outside by the pool, eating breakfast. I could sense Shake was feeling uneasy. He appeared to be nervous and uncomfortable. He looked at me and said, "Deeps, I don't think we will work out."

My stomach immediately sank. I knew it was my physical appearance and our intimate moments. That was a problem for him. It was my intuition telling me because he didn't explicitly say that he didn't like my body. He just said that it wouldn't work out with us. I knew I shouldn't care what somebody else thought of me. But caring what others thought of me was instilled in my brain since childhood. It's hard to overcome these thoughts when you are so emotionally charged. Retraining your brain on the spot takes practice, and I was in no state of mind to comfort myself.

I could feel my heart breaking. I knew I possessed all the qualities to be a good wife for him and saw the bigger picture with us. I thought, *Maybe it will take him some time to realize that we are good for each other*. I was able to get him to perceive situations differently; the pods were evidence of that. And, so I thought if he genuinely got to know me as a person, he would see my worth, and the physical connection would follow.

I pushed through and kept that poker face. I rarely ever cry in front of others, and there was no chance I'd ever let Shake think his words impacted me. I liked to play the cool girl. I took a few deep breaths to control my racing heart. I could have left at any moment, but I wanted to give it my all to prove to him and myself that I was worthy. It was the most intense roller-coaster of emotions.

As Shake expressed his doubts to me, I could tell he was highly anxious. I knew I had to be a friend to him at this moment. I had to help him objectively sort through his racing thoughts. I calmed him down and explained that this was all a process. It *is* scary; marriage is a lifelong promise—that is not a commitment I take lightly. I talked to him about removing the pressure from the situation, being ourselves, and having fun. If our relationship didn't lead to a marriage, that's okay. That is precisely what this experiment was about, I explained to him. It's about seeing whether you can fall in love this way and whether it could lead to a happy marriage.

I know what you must be thinking. How could I stay with someone that told me they didn't see a future with me? I wish I knew the answer to that. Why did you not just walk away? Sometimes, I wish I had. But I was attracted to Shake even though he wasn't my usual physical type. We had built a connection, and, in my mind, we were already connected in a way no one else would understand. It surprised me that I felt this way. Why did I care about him so much already?

I explained to Shake that if we chose not to marry each other at the end of this experience, we at least tried exploring the connection. I have witnessed firsthand in my parents' arranged marriage that you can grow in your love for someone over time. I knew I would be a great friend, wife, mother, and lover. Maybe if we spent more time together, he would see it too.

Perhaps a part of me stayed because I thought he would fall in love with me. If he only got to know me better and see my soul, he would envision building this empire we discussed in the pods. My whole life, I was a people pleaser because I wanted to be liked, and I knew I over-compensated in my love life for this reason. This is a quality I have been trying to stray from, but it feels like it's been etched into my bones in a way that it can never heal. I make a conscious effort to change this part of me because it only leads to me emptying my cup and, unfortunately, it often falls into the hands of someone unworthy.

After that conversation, Shake seemed to become much more relaxed. He started to ease up. He put on some music, and we had the best day just dancing while enjoying each other's company. We took cute pictures of us kissing by the pool, and I cherished our sweet moments from that day. That wasn't the last of our fun times together in Mexico. Yes, there were some instances where I could see a side of him that I didn't like, but the good ones overpowered them.

The next morning, we were going to film a couple of scenes. I specifically remember Shake making a comment that upset me. When the crew returned to film, he looked at one of the team members and said, "Oh, look at her; she's so cute. That's my type of girl." That comment reminded me that this man did not have a filter regarding his thoughts. It shocked me that he lacked the self-awareness to know that he shouldn't make comments like that to his fiancée. That was when I started seeing more slight hints of his true character. They were being dropped everywhere like little stink bombs.

During our Mexico excursions, we got along well, and I could see a genuine friendship blossoming. I thought, *At least I can say I found a good friend out of this situation.* Secretly, I was hoping to extract more goodness from him as I did in the pods. Friendship was a good place to start, and we were building on top of the emotional foundation that was already cemented.

On one occasion, Shake was raving about cenotes and how cool they were. I had never heard of a cenote before. He explained to me that a cenote was a sinkhole that exposed groundwater. I was very excited to try something new with him because it would give Shake a chance to see me in a different light. After all, I loved adventures, travel, and exploring new cities. Jumping into a cenote was now on my bucket list. (Yes, I added it to my bucket list a few hours after learning about it). I was getting to have a new experience in a magical way with Shake, and I was thrilled.

We listened to Kygo (an EDM artist), the entire van ride to the cenote, which was about two hours, there and back. That day was one of the best days I'd had with Shake. It was light-hearted, fun, and thrilling. He saw me through a different lens and even vocalized it to me. His compliment made me feel seen and encouraged. While laying on hammocks after our excursion, he kissed me and said he was excited to go back to Chicago and live with me. Maybe he was starting to see me as more than just a friend.

Meeting the other castmates in Mexico was one of the best moments of filming. I was genuinely curious to see what everyone looked like and to talk to the girls again. They were my safety blankets; I knew them way better than Shake or any other guys. The hosts, Vanessa and Nick, were a big blessing too. They were kind and intrigued to get an update from us outside the pods. It was easy to talk to them, and they had been married for years, so their advice was appreciated.

Shake once again said something inappropriate regarding how good Vanessa looked, leaving me with another dagger of doubt. *Could he really be this shallow?* I wondered. I could sense Nick being uncomfortable with his comment, but he let it roll off his back, as a classy man does. It was hard to believe Shake would say such things because of how kind and sensitive he was with me.

Although alcohol was involved during our time in Mexico, it wasn't like we were drunk all the time. I questioned why I got stuck with a man that didn't consider my feelings. Or was he just so oblivious to the fact that it impacted me? I never did vocalize it, but I felt like I didn't want to. I wanted to see who he was without me shaping his thoughts. This brought up my past feelings of rejection and the longing to crawl out of my skin again. I wanted to be the woman he loved completely. This time, however, I wasn't willing to change myself or wish I was someone else. I was proud of my inner thoughts, and I gave myself grace. I knew

I had a lot to offer, and I had faith that Shake would eventually start to see that.

Later that evening, I eagerly awaited the arrival of all the couples. I specifically remember being excited to meet Kyle. He was my number two person in the pods. Kyle and I had many dates, which made me curious about him. To my disappointment, the hosts told me he was not coming. There was a COVID scare, and Shaina and Kyle were quarantined in their room. Seeing the couples and putting faces to the names of the guys I'd been talking to was exciting. It was odd to hear the same voices I had heard in the pods; it was an experience unlike any other. I got along very well with all the guys, and we all had a good time and had chances to speak with each other.

Out of the corner of my eye, I could see Shake getting animated as he talked. I could tell he was drunk, but I had no idea what he was saying. Later that night, Shake and I continued to bond intimately. Still, at this time I was completely unaware of the inappropriate words he had spoken hours before. Later I discovered he was not speaking highly of me, and I heard exactly what he said when the show aired.

On our way home to Chicago, we could finally check our phones. This was like Christmas morning—we had been without external contact for almost three weeks. The first thing most of us did was look everyone up on Instagram. Several followers became the determining factor of popularity. I didn't care what I posted on Instagram, let alone how many followers or likes I had. But it seemed evident that it mattered to Shake. I only had around a thousand followers. My circle was small. After all, I wasn't a DJ meeting people every weekend.

My parents lived two hours away and I no longer had an apartment in the city. This meant living in an apartment with Shake while we continued filming and planning our wedding—an extremely peculiar concept that somehow still felt normal.

Moving into our apartment in Chicago was easy. One, it was a beautiful space surrounded by glass windows overlooking Navy Pier on the lake and the city. And two, because at this point, we were getting along and bonding as our experiences intertwined. This was a new space for both of us. We later visited Shake's condo as well but lived in the two-bedroom apartment during the filming.

Moving in with Shake was an integral part of the growth of our relationship, and living with him was reasonably easy. I worked from home, and he would have long days at the vet's office, so I made dinner and took care of Bandit, his dog. I loved that little guy; he gave me unconditional love and was the perfect addition to the apartment. Shake was impressed that I could cook, and I would even pack him lunches for work.

I tried to make life easy on him because it was stressful for him to go to work and film at the same time. When I tell you I pour all my energy into relationships, I do. Making other people happy makes me happier than making myself happy, and I have identified this as another problem. I tend to give too much in a relationship. Shake didn't have much time or the mental capacity to do much for me. I tried to

justify it by telling myself that I had more flexibility than
him with my work schedule, so that's why he was less likely
to be present for me. We slept in the same bed, but
cuddling was the extent of our intimacy at this point. I still
valued that. I never liked to initiate anything sexually
because I liked to match my partner's energy. I liked when
my partner wanted me, and since Shake lacked physical
chemistry with me, I matched that. But he would tell me in
the mornings before work that I made it hard for him to
leave the bed because we were so cozy cuddling together.
This was my favorite form of intimacy with him. We barely
even kissed anymore. Sometimes, it would feel like we were
an old married couple— comfortable.

It was almost time to meet the parents. This was the
first time in my entire thirty years of existence that I would
bring home a guy to my parents. This made me feel
extremely uneasy. I hated talking about intimacy or relationships with my parents. The thought of it made me
cringe. But as Shake entered our home, it was evident he
got along well with my family. He was respectful to my
parents and knew the names of all the Indian food my
parents made for him. This part of the cultural similarities
made it easy for him to connect to my family. It was almost
too easy.

My parents questioned us about what we wanted out of
this situation. Marriage in this fashion (on a reality TV
show) was unheard of for my parents' generation, especially how they grew up. My parents told Shake how they
had met and the trajectory of their relationship. It was the
first time I heard them talk about their relationship. My dad
spoke of how much he loved my mom. They got an

arranged marriage, and my mom expressed how much my dad meant to her. She shared her gratitude for his support and kind nature. This conversation brought tears to my eyes, and I could see Shake was bonding with my family. This made me like him even more. It was wild to me that he fit into the family so well. I've only dated two white men my whole life, and I was beginning to understand how being of the same race could make relationships a little easier.

On the drive home from my parents that night, I felt a stronger connection to Shake. We were getting even more comfortable with each other. It was easy to talk to him, and while there was a lot I held back, there was also a lot that I shared with him. Going back to our apartment and laying down next to him at night was something I enjoyed. It was familiar, and I felt like we were together. We were building a foundation. At the very least, we had a friendship that I thought would last forever. I enjoyed taking care of him when he was stressed. I found happiness in making his life easier when he was working because I knew the pressure he was under. He talked to me about not finding joy in his job anymore and was thinking about making a career change. I supported his decision to want something better for himself. He shared so many of his thoughts and ideas with me on what he wanted to do. He wanted to take many paths, and it was clear he was confused about solidifying a resolution for this part of his life. But he knew he could lean on me to talk it through logically.

Next, it was time to meet his side of the family in a few days. Shake's family was small because he was an only child. We discussed this aspect of his life and how he wished he had siblings to lean on. Parents don't understand what you're going through the same way siblings do. Siblings are your best friends who tend to give you the harsh truth. It made me think about my relationship with my siblings and how much I relied on their advice and love.

When we discussed this, I reassured Shake that he would always have my brother, sister, and sister-in-law in his corner. He felt like family now because we spent so much time together. And when I would talk to Sunny about what Shake was trying to do career-wise, Sunny told me he openly gave Shake any advice he was willing to listen to. They spoke of Shake potentially going into IT, although this was a challenging field to break into. My brother was a friend to him, and they had a lot of similarities, such as their love for the same type of music. I liked that they were also building a relationship because that was something that I had never experienced with my previous boyfriends. Well, the truth is, I never gave Sunny the chance to get to know them, either.

When the day arrived to meet Shake's family, I was extremely nervous. This was not an ordinary situation, and Shake did so well with my family that there was added pressure to ensure I had the same experience. On top of it all, it would be filmed. All of this was hard, but I knew I just had to be myself. It wasn't surprising that meeting his parents and loving them was the easiest thing to do. They were kind and welcoming, and I felt like I was in my own home. The energy they exuded was familiar and very similar to my own.

They gave us endearing advice on relationships which I truly appreciated. My parents had an arranged marriage, and it was full of love. Shake's parents had what's called a "love-marriage" in the Indian culture. Their relationship already had a foundation of love before they got married. So, their advice and experiences were different from that of my parents. It was refreshing to talk to them, and I loved our visit. They said, "You will never find the perfect person. You just have to see if someone's flaws are worth living with." They went on to say compatibility is essential.

I couldn't believe how easy integrating into Shake's family was. They were such wonderful people, and I could genuinely see them being part of my life. Meeting Shake's family only reinforced how much potential there could be between us and made me want this engagement with Shake to work. I felt he was also impacted by us meeting each other's families. There's something compelling about seeing how someone could fit within your family circle. But, in the back of my mind, all I could think about was how much importance he placed on dating a certain kind of girl—the type of girl who looked nothing like me.

During that next week, I was waiting for Shake to wake up one day and change his mind. As we cuddled in bed together and he pulled me closer, I hoped he would start to see me differently because of the growing emotional connections. I soon realized it didn't matter what I did; it would never change. I began to see him in a different light. There would be small things he would do that would annoy me. It was in how he spoke about things; it was sometimes negative. I understood he was stressed, but I was tired of giving and not getting anything back. I would wait to see if he would kiss me or make a move. It never happened, and I didn't try either because I could read his body language. Again, I tend to match the energy I get in any relationship.

When planning our wedding, he emphasized the "party" aspect. He wanted to throw the perfect party for his friends, one they would remember forever. I had no idea what he was saying in interviews when I was not around, but I remember one day, when he got home from one, he said, "Deeps, you would be proud of me. I'm taking a different approach in my interviews now."

I honestly have no idea what he meant by that, but my intuition told me it wasn't anything good. I wished I could be a fly in that interview room wall.

One night, Shake had a friend's birthday party to attend, and he got all dressed up in a suit. I was on the couch cuddling with his dog, ready to have a chill night. He came into the living room, putting his socks on, and said, "It must be killing you."

I replied, "What must be killing me?" I had no idea where he was going with this.

He followed, "You know, it must be killing you to see me dressed like this, and you're not even able to come with me."

At that moment, something changed in me. I was annoyed that he thought so highly of himself. I didn't vocalize it at the time, but I was so turned off. It was not so much the words he uttered but his demeanor when he said them. I was starting to see a shift in the way I saw him.

Even then, there were fun moments we shared. The next day, we got on a call with both of our moms. They were helping us plan the wedding because neither Shake nor I knew what it took to plan an Indian wedding. We had a blast that night talking to our moms. We would put ourselves on mute at times and just crack up laughing, listening to them talk. These were the moments that left me confused because, on the one hand, I disliked certain character traits in him, but we always found a way to have fun. The emotions I felt came in waves of good and bad.

During our bachelor and bachelorette parties, a lot more information came to the surface. My conversation with Iyanna on the boat was eye-opening because, unlike before, I could finally talk about my feelings. Her words of advice made me realize that I shouldn't have to fight for someone to see my worth. If he couldn't know I would be a great wife to him, it was his loss. Why was I fighting to prove myself?

Later that night, I got even more blinding news. The parties combined, and the women and men came together for an after-party at Danielle and her fiancé, Nick's apartment. Shake had to work in the morning, so he went back to our apartment to sleep.

Later that night, Jarrette, Iynanna's fiancé, pulled me aside to talk in the hallway. He warned me that Shake didn't speak highly of me in Mexico. Granted, we were still getting to know each other at that point, but apparently, Shake said things about my physical appearance, which left an uneasy feeling in my stomach. This information, paired with hints from Shayne, another man from the pods, on how Shake used his words, was very telling of Shake's character. I knew I wasn't getting the real Shake. He was "on his best" behavior around me and was a completely different person around the guys behind my back.

Even with this intel, we continued seeing each other because a whole team was planning our Indian wedding which would be filmed. My mindset was shifting, though, and I saw the situation for what it was. It concerned me that Shake was saying things behind my back. I was told that he told other castmates that I was a "Houdini with makeup." At that moment, I took this as a compliment because I didn't care for makeup that much. I was a simple girl. I did the bare minimum. I turned it up when I needed to.

Trying on my wedding dress made me feel bittersweet. The outcome of this wedding would not end in a marriage, and it couldn't. With only days left till the altar, in my mind, I already knew how this would end. Even so, I at least thought I had made a friend through this experience because of the unique experience we had gone through. Shake was getting excited about this "party" we were planning. In his mind, it wasn't even a wedding. He was initially going to be wearing a suit along with his groomsmen. So, I decided just to put my bridesmaids in dresses.

One day he was shopping with the guys, and I got a call from him saying, "Hey, I changed my mind; I am going to wear Indian attire." Through his conversations with friends, I think Shake realized that he wanted to show the Indian culture more and tried to embrace it. I might be giving him too much credit, but I'd like to think that is why he chose to do this and not the fact that he would look cool.

This moment was highly frustrating for me because my girls had already bought their dresses. With such short notice, I had no idea how I would pull together Indian outfits for my bridesmaids. This was another telling sign that all Shake cared about was himself. He didn't have the awareness or mental capacity to think from others' perspectives. My mom, Divya, and Hina drove to Chicago the next day for me. We went to Devon Street and spent all day trying to find all the pieces we needed for this wedding day that I knew wouldn't even end in a marriage.

I expressed to Shake how much time and effort it took to do this. It was easy for men because they just threw on an outfit. For the girls, you must find a blouse that fits them and match saris, jewelry, and shoes. It was an arduous task to accomplish in such a short period of time. I would not have been able to do it without my family. I wouldn't have been able to get through most of this Shake experience without them. His lack of understanding infuriated me, and I began to enjoy my time without him when he was working. I could finally relax and be myself, something I couldn't do when he was around. I stopped seeing him with rose-colored glasses and saw his lack of empathy in how he talked to others around us.

Shake and I couldn't see each other for a couple of days before the wedding. This was the time that I was truly able to reflect on our experience. On the one hand, I was sad that it was ending, but on the other, I was ready to move forward from a stuck situation. The words kept replaying in my head of how Shake wanted to DJ and throw the most epic party for his friends and celebrate. I, too, wanted to celebrate a friendship. But in the later months, I realized we were both trying to celebrate two completely different things. He didn't care about me; it was all about how he would come off to his friends. Shake may have had the potential to be a husband, but the night before the wedding, I realized that he did not possess any of the qualities I was looking for in *my* future husband.

There was no chance that I could say yes to him at the altar. He once said out loud to our producer in front of me,

"If you give me this apartment for a year, I'll marry Deepti." All the pieces had added up, and it was apparent Shake didn't care for me. He was putting on an act so that he would continue being in my good graces. I still cared for him despite my many revelations and his skewed mentality. I knew that there was good in him. He couldn't fake it this much, or so I thought.

The wedding day was a tough one for me. I kept thinking of the perfect words to say to him that day when I would see him for the first time after a couple of days. Getting ready was hard because I was getting my hair and makeup done for a bittersweet day. My friends were here supporting me, not knowing what I was going through. Some had even flown in from other States thinking this would be the happiest day of my life. My parents would see me in my wedding outfit, knowing this was not the special day they had thought it would be. But I had to get through it with pride, dignity, and elegance. Even if I disliked many aspects of the person I would meet at the altar, I couldn't embarrass or demean him in any way. *I had to choose myself.*

Before walking down the aisle, I kept replaying what I wanted to say in my head. I was overcome with nervousness and just wanted to get it over with. Of course, there was no way I could say yes to someone who didn't see me for me. How could I? If things had been different and Shake's mindset had changed, maybe my answer would be different; I can't fully know because he never did show that his love for me was growing. I deserved someone who knew for sure. This is a marriage. I couldn't be with someone like Shake. Someone who says to me, "I don't feel an animalistic, instinctual attraction to you," is certainly not husband material. Those words creep me out, honestly. But I guess he was a veterinarian, so these kinds of words were in his vocabulary. Actually, I think that makes it even creepier.

I looked back on Shake's and my love story on that day. It was unique and ours, and I wanted to celebrate that I may have at least gotten a friend from this scenario. I knew I could never marry him, but we created a unique bond with everything we had gone through. It was special to me, as fucked up as that sounds. Yes, there are many qualities I did not like about him, but we had formed great memories together, and that was meaningful to me. I wanted to celebrate that. He wanted to celebrate his moment to shine with his friends. He saw this as a party in which he was the main character. I didn't realize that till later.

As I walked down the aisle in anticipation, it comforted me to know that my dad was by my side and that my friends and family were sitting there in support. I had people to lean on for comfort. The first thing Shake said to me after I walked down the aisle was, "Wow, you look so hot."

I already knew what I would say at the altar, but his words just further confirmed that he was not my person. It was how he told them to me, as if I were an object, not a person. I can't explain it because some of you reading this might think these are sweet words. But, to me, they were gross. He did follow it up at the altar later with, "You look beautiful," but those earlier words just stuck to me like glue. And in those moments waiting for my turn to speak, I knew exactly what I wanted to say.

The exact words still ring in my head: "Abhi, I hope you know how much you mean to me and the impact that you have made on my life. But, no, I cannot marry you. I deserve someone who knows for sure. So, I am choosing myself, and I'm going to say no."

I knew that he wasn't the one for me. If he were, he would have made me feel like I was the one. He never did that, not once. That moment made me realize I could see the hurt in his eyes. The hurt came because he was rejected in front of everyone, not because he lost me. I could see now that he didn't respond well to that. He knew all along what both of our answers were going to be, but he didn't get a chance to speak at the altar. I walked away after my answer.

It hurts to watch it back, and I have only watched it once because after I left, Shake told the guests that he would've said "no" but didn't want to embarrass me. He also said he was a little upset, but overall, it was a net positive—as if I was a transaction. How could he not recognize that as inappropriate? It further proves that his intentions that day were just to party and have a good time. Even if he saw no physical connection, he could at least reflect that it would have been amazing if it had worked out. He could show emotion that he was at least sad that everything was changing between us yet again, but he didn't care enough to think about me.

After the ceremony, I was gone for most of my "wedding reception." My mom came and spoke with me. I was hurt inside because I did want to find my person, my love. It could have been with Shake because many parts of our lives could intertwine beautifully. The biggest blessing of my life was Shake's uncertainty because otherwise, I might have considered being married to a man who lacked most qualities I was looking for in a husband and, indeed, even a friend. However, I wouldn't let my mom see my sadness because I knew this was all for the best. Things always have a way of working out. Rejection is redirection.

It hurt me to see my mom cry; I never want to see that. She was my rock, and her support meant so much to me. I reassured her that I was fine; I chose myself. To hear her say, "I'm proud of you, I just want you to be happy," at that moment were the exact words I needed to hear. Here she was again, there for me through every difficult moment of life. "That's my brave girl, my sweetheart," she said. I knew I was going to be okay. I had her, my family, and my friends. She knew all the complications I was having with Shake. She knew that I wasn't going to marry him. She wouldn't have approved of it even if I did. She and Hina had their reservations from the start. She expected more from him, as I did. He didn't deserve me.

Almost a year after filming, I already started to see a different side to Shake that I did not like. I honestly tried to be friends with him, but I did not want to be around his self-absorbed energy. Not only did I witness many of his negative behaviors, but I heard many awful stories revealing his true character. By the time the show aired, I wasn't speaking to him, and was ignoring most of his texts to me.

Once the show aired, I got to see an even darker side of Shake. All I could think watching it back was that this was *not* the person I had cared for. This version of Shake talking to the cameras and castmates was someone completely different.

I think one of the parts that hurt me most was the scene on our wedding day after I had said my piece and left the altar. I had assumed that Shake might have been saddened by how our story ended. I thought maybe it had meant something to him. But all I could see was someone who was in this experience for himself and who clearly did not have my best interests at heart during any part of the process.

I honestly didn't care that Shake wasn't physically attracted to me. It's important for me to acknowledge that. You cannot have a marriage where there isn't intimacy. We both deserved to find that in a partner. What I don't respect in him is how he acts and engages with those around him. He values only those with physical beauty, a major social platform, and those who agree with his male chauvinistic mentality.

Shake's behavior and interactions since the show aired have been nothing short of vindictive. I think he must have realized quickly that he really fucked up with how he handled himself on the show. It's hard to imagine that he felt he could say such horrible things about people and that nobody would mind. And unfortunately, Shake has channeled his anger and embarrassment into trying to attack everyone around him.

I can see it in his eyes when I see videos of him; he's not the same person I cared for a year ago. He has hatred in his heart. His words are a projection of his insecurities. Resentment has his judgment clouded. He's jealous of others' successes and bitter that the cast has built meaningful relationships beyond him. That's the only sensible explanation for why he continues to try to tear so many people down, even though we have all moved on from him.

When I learned that Shake could not be trusted as a friend, I set boundaries to protect myself. I stopped picking up his calls, and I stopped responding to his texts. I also blocked him on social media. Enough was enough, and I would not be used as a pawn in his vie for attention.

I felt compelled to write this chapter and share more about my journey with Shake because I wanted the opportunity to speak my truth. I've remained quiet about many of the awful things he has had to say about me, my family, and my friends since the show aired, mainly because I didn't want to encourage or invite that kind of negativity in my life.

Long after the show aired, I did my best not to speak badly about him—even though he clearly never had that commitment to me. In my interviews, I tell people we need to be kind because, for someone to grow, reflect and change their inappropriate behaviors, they need a positive environment. When the flower starts to fade, you don't change the flower; you change its environment. I was trying to spread good while he continued being a villain. He continues pointing fingers at the cast and saying *he* is the victim. But it's actually the complete opposite—we weren't bullying him; we were all standing up to a bully.

I now realize that part of choosing myself is having the courage to stand up for myself and the people I love and care about. I was raised on good values: be uplifting, inspiring, and a life-changer. I literally took those words to heart since childhood. These values are what make life worthwhile. They bond us together in humanity, and they push us to continue to do better. Even if someone doesn't always see the best in me, I've always tried to see the best in them.

And unlike Shake, I have been able to acknowledge the good in our relationship and appreciate it for what it was. No one person or experience is all bad—there is always something to learn.

The truth is, we all have things we need to work on, and we always will. Even with this understanding, the responsibility to fix someone else doesn't fall on our shoulders—that's on the other person. I think this was probably my greatest lesson from being with Shake; I realized that for far too long, I had been someone who tried to fix the guys around me. And in the process, I had often lost myself.

But with Shake, I finally learned to take a stand and say enough is enough. We have every right to set boundaries for ourselves and to protect our energy from those who do not wish us well. Shake continues to live in the past, and I'm choosing to live in the present and move on.

My lesson is this: trust yourself. Don't worry if others have your back or what they think of you. The opinions of others do not define your reality. Know your worth, and don't settle for anything less than extraordinary. Trust deeply, in your mind and your heart, that you can succeed in love and life, and you absolutely will.

KYLE GETS DEEP

"People come into your life for a
reason, a season, or a lifetime."
– Brian A. "Drew" Chalker.

The days after my wedding were tough for me, I
didn't have a place in Chicago, and all I wanted to
do was spend time with the new friends I had
made. I met with Danielle, and we went out to Old Town,
Chicago. I stayed the night with her, and she didn't know
how much that meant to me. I had her support and knew
she would always have my back. I'll never forget that day
because she understood what I was going through and that
it was hard. She made sure that I was comfortable. She said,
"Deepti, when I first saw you, you were sitting on your suitcase at the airport, and I remember thinking, *Wow, she is so
pretty.*"

At that moment, I realized that other women felt the
same emotions I did. They had insecurities of their own
they were dealing with. Hearing something as simple as

that from her was oddly comforting, and having her uncon-ditional love meant everything to me.

Sunday, I met Shake at Nobu (he really did have reser-vations) along with Vito, another castmate. I wanted to see what our interactions would be like now. Again, I tried to maintain a friendship. This was all before knowing all the vile things he had said about me to castmates, producers, and of course on camera—which, as previously described, I would only find out about a year later. Shake wasn't with us for long. He took selfie-style pictures of us together, had a drink, and left. It felt odd to me that he wanted to take pictures together even though it seemed like he wasn't very interested in catching up. Vito and I continued our conver-sation alone, and it was apparent that Shake was eager to return to his own life. He was already starting to feel like a stranger.

That night, I drove back home to my parents' home. It felt strange being there after everything that had happened. I leaned on my family and my best friend, Laura. She was my escape because I could freely talk to her about anything. She was a soon-to-be mother, and watching her grow throughout her marriage and pregnancy, gave her wisdom. My friends' lives were changing before my eyes, and I couldn't help but reflect on mine. Here I was, going through something so crazy and trying to return to normalcy. But "getting back to normal" just seemed unat-tainable, at least right then.

After a week at home, I started looking for apartments. I wanted to be back in Chicago. People from the cast were hanging out, and I wanted to be a part of that. It was around that time that I reached out to Kyle. I got his number from

Sal. He was on my mind because I had a strong connection with him that ended abruptly after the pods. You see, you tend to form strong feelings with more than one person during the dating process within the pods. It's crazy to think I spent almost the same amount of time with Kyle as I did with Shake.

I envisioned a life with Kyle at a high level, but much of it was a mystery to me. I wasn't sure how we'd raise our kids, how our families would interact. All I knew was that life would be the best adventure with him. I loved his wittiness and his love for banter. He intellectually stimulated me, and I could have different types of deep conversations with him than I could with the other guys. I craved that exact type of relationship, one that challenged my perspective. He knew my connection with Shake was strong in the pods, which made him uneasy. As a result, his drive to want to connect with me lessened as our dates went on. He said, "If we wanted to be engaged, you have to ask me." But I didn't want to do that. I wanted him to be sure and have *him* ask me. He didn't know how hard it was for me to choose Shake over him. It was an internal struggle for me, but he decided on our behalf. He chose Caitlin and Shaina as his top two women. This upset me, but I never let anyone know that. I just accepted it.

I still remember my first text to him on June 17, 2021, where I wrote:

At some point in life, we must meet.

His response was immediate:

Give me a time and place.

I didn't think he had my number, so I questioned how

he knew it was me. His comeback to my question was clever:

I didn't have to dig too DEEP to figure it out.

This made me smile. On our pod dates, we loved puns. We would incorporate them throughout our encounters. That's how he became my "Kylesaurus"—this nickname for him is still listed on my phone to this day.

It was just so easy to talk to Kyle. We texted back and forth about our experiences. He wondered what it would have been like had he chosen differently. He said he had regrets. I thought about this too. How different would it have been if Kyle and I chose each other? We were both still processing what had happened. It was odd to think I dated him in the pods and that he was so close to being my number one person. When we discussed this, he said, "I know, I know, I fucked up." There was no time to think this way because we'd drive ourselves crazy into madness, harping on the 'what-ifs.'

I was left disappointed in my apartment search. There were none available immediately. Some were available in July, but that seemed so far away. I needed an escape right now. I got on the phone with my childhood best friend, Derek. He told me to come to LA to stay with him for a while. My mom encouraged me to go because she knew I wasn't myself. She could see that I needed a break from this place. She told me I looked like there was no life in me. She was used to my bubbly nature, and in my current state, I was completely numb, just trying to process everything. I didn't want to sit with the hurt and the memories for too long.

So, I decided to go to LA for almost a month. It was the

exact thing I needed. Derek and his roommates were there for me in such a special way. After all, he was a psychologist. He, of course, had his regular patients and didn't even realize he was taking on another one—me. LA was the perfect distraction. I worked remotely from there. Derek and I would work out in the mornings, get freshly squeezed juice and turmeric shots, and then work. We played tennis, went to Dodgers games, and had fun night outs. He was my ultimate best friend when I needed him the most. I am so thankful for that time with him. It was the space and distance I needed to run from everything and breathe in a new place.

I remember being upset with Shake for how he used his social media during this time. Only a couple of weeks after wrapping up filming, he posted Instagram stories of his dates with other girls. He would post these bizarrely cropped images of girls showing only their boobs and drinks, and I found this to be completely distasteful. I again saw his true colors.

In those first few months fresh off the show, Shake was always eager to plan group activities with the cast; I missed a few at the start. He started flirting with other women from the cast in our group chats. He even took one on a date. I didn't mind that this was happening; it just could have been done in a conversation I wasn't present in. These were the little jabs he would take. I am unsure if he was trying to make me jealous or just lacked the self-awareness to care about my perspective.

While I was out in LA, Kyle and I continued our texting. He told me about how the group hangs went. We had very flirtatious energy. We would joke and have witty comebacks. I enjoyed talking to him and wanted to meet him in person, finally. I had been trying to meet Kyle since we returned to Chicago. When I was engaged to Shake, I remember thinking that I had wanted to see what Kyle looked like in person. I was never granted that chance. Kyle knew I was looking for a place to live, and he even started to help me look. This was the best part about him; he was always eager to help. I was going to be in Chicago for the Fourth of July, and we talked about meeting that weekend.

We both had an attraction to each other, and I was drawn to him. I loved the way he spoke; that's all I could even remember of him from the pods—his voice. We somehow didn't end up meeting that weekend.

I did have a chance to meet with a few others. Caitlin and I scheduled a dinner date when I was visiting Chicago. That dinner was so special to me because she asked how I was doing, unlike some of the other castmates who were more focused on the gossip. I could quickly identify who truly cared for me and not the clout of the show. She wasn't there to get the inside scoop. She was there for me; it was easy to see that she cared. We didn't need to only talk about the show or what happened. There were other important aspects to life too. This friendship was special to me. I saw the type of person she was and decided that this was someone I wanted in my life.

Shake arranged a meetup for all the cast; it was a yacht party to see fireworks. By then, I had already found an apartment and moved into it. I was excited about this. It was the first time I would see everyone since the show wrapped. I was excited to see the girls again, but mostly, I was excited to see Kyle for the first time.

We met up at Caitlin's place first before going to the boat. I was hoping Kyle would come, but he didn't. After getting to the boat, he still wasn't there. I was sure he wasn't coming, considering we had already left the dock. After some time had passed, I remember walking from the front of the boat to the back, and there he was. He was talking to Joey, Caitlin's fiancé at the time. I remember looking at him and feeling excited to hear his voice again. He arrived on his jet ski to the boat. Yeah, of course, I liked that.

That was a fun night, but the other girls on the boat were attractive. Kyle did not shy away from talking to everyone. I was in a peculiar headspace, too. As much as I was into Kyle, I was anxious about Shake and our situation. I later found out that Kyle had met someone he liked on the boat outside of the cast. I didn't know that at the time, so we just continued to text like we usually did; we were friends just starting to get to know each other outside this crazy experience we had been through.

A couple of weeks later, Shake arranged another get-together at his friend's penthouse. It was Lollapalooza weekend and Shake and I discussed seeing one of our favorite artists, Illenium. I would speak with Shake occasionally, but it wasn't as consistent as I was talking with Kyle. Shake and I left early that night to go to the show. I was left heavily disappointed because Shake was not fully present with me. He took a couple of videos and left me there alone. He said, "I think I'm going to get out of here early to avoid the rush later. You going to be okay by yourself?"

At that moment, I saw that he wasn't even a good friend. It honestly made me regret leaving Kyle at the penthouse party. I was enjoying talking to him finally. And I went with someone who didn't even care about me. It felt like he was there to get content for his Instagram, and when he got it, he left. Every time I hung out with Shake alone, I felt disappointed. He became more of an acquaintance that I would only see in group settings.

I tried to see Kyle later that weekend at the festival. But Grant Park was huge, and I lost reception; a meetup didn't end up happening. Over the next few weeks, Hope (another castmate), Caitlin, and I grew very close. I also hung out with Danielle a lot. Time was flying, and it was already the end of August. The friendships from this show were of so much value to me. We showed up for each other, and for that reason alone, I'd do the show a hundred times over again and go through all the pain.

We planned another group hangout at Hope's place this time. Many of the cast were there, and that night, Kyle and I were especially flirtatious. He gave me a ride on his moped to the bar. And, afterward, he drove me home. That was the night of our first kiss. I was hesitant at first. But it felt right. It was the sweetest, most tender kiss. Almost too innocent. That was what made it special to me. Our lips touched so softly, and I remember feeling all the feels over it. There was a part of me that was holding back. I didn't want to get into anything too soon. We texted each other almost every day from then on. I would hang out mostly with him and the girls. There were no dull moments. I made new friends too. I loved this new chapter of my life in Chicago.

I must admit that I'm often guilty of letting my past relationships dictate what I expect in the future. I will try to size up a new person by comparing them to my exes, and in doing so, I lose out on someone who might be great for me.

These days, I try not to do that. I take a chance and open myself up to just one person at a time. And that's been working well for me.

Or so I thought until Kyle showed up.

"Old habits die hard."

Gosh, whoever said that, wasn't kidding. I slid back into codependent behavior even after all the stuff I'd gone through.

Here's what I mean.

When I first started to hang out with Kyle, it was very innocent. We were magnetized to each other in group gatherings and naturally gravitated toward one another. Our friendship began in earnest when we both sensed something between us. I would look for him in crowds and always wanted to be around his energy. There was a pull to him. When I would accidently graze his arm, I felt euphoric. It was odd because I still wouldn't say I liked showing him that I had feelings. I loved being flirtatious but didn't want to fall into that next level—love. In the back of my head, I was thinking about what people might say. Yes, I know; sometimes, I fall into that old trap of wondering what others think about me. The show hadn't even aired yet, and what if I had romantic feelings for someone else from the cast?

I was still not too fond of expressing my emotions to romantic partners. I expected them to pick up on my physical cues—nonverbal communication matters to me. I know this is a learned behavior, but I don't particularly like putting myself out there for fear of rejection. That fear lingers, but at least I've identified this in my life, and when those thoughts come up, I'm ready for them.

So, I throw feelers out there to see if the guys I'm interested in, gravitate toward me. Kyle did just that. It was effortless because getting up and going with him was easy. At first, we hung out in groups—sometimes large groups of people and sometimes in fours. Slowly, it started to dwindle to just the two of us. I loved those moments.

We would do ordinary things together and sometimes extraordinary things. We'd pick out plants and replant them in our favorite pots. We would go on a boat and cruise on the lake with his best friends. Our conversations would last hours on end and feel like minutes. We had intellectual talks about our interests, past relationships, and the world. Simple chats like what the universe was like and our different understandings of the purpose of life.

Kyle was practical, and I was spiritual. I valued his perspectives on it. Though I would disagree, it fascinated me that he was capable enough to challenge my thinking. I reciprocated the challenge. You see, I like to be right about everything. I know I'm not, yet I try to say things confidently, and most of the time, my intuition about something is correct. Who am I to argue with those odds?

The seasons started to change, and one of the only constants became Kyle. There was no commitment between us, but I had lots of emotional passion for him, and I couldn't get him out of my head. He was the first person I would text in the morning and the last at night. It was so effortless to carry on a conversation. I was still hesitant to vocalize my feelings, and he was not ready for a relationship. He didn't have to tell me that; his actions spoke for themselves. I'd rather have a friendship than ruin it by expressing my feelings, I thought. I knew this wasn't healthy. But I also knew that he cared for me and had feelings too. And, again, he didn't have to tell me; he showed me. I felt his loving energy through his actions. Acts of service were his love language.

We started to get comfortable with each other, and he was my best friend after almost two months of hanging out. I had feelings for Kyle already, and I knew he did for me. But we were both single and free to do whatever we wanted, and I knew that Kyle was seeing other women, and I was going on a few dates with others, too. Even though this was the case, I would always think of Kyle. He set the bar high.

I loved his dog, Linus. We called him Liney. Sometimes I'd watch him when Kyle was at work. Liney was the best coworker. It was clear that Kyle and I were building a friendship, and there was undoubtedly chemistry there. One night, we were on his boat, and he invited one of his other female friends. I could see that between their interactions, they were extremely flirty. I cried that night because watching him with someone else was hard. In the back of my mind, I knew we were free to do whatever we wanted and weren't rushing into anything. Plus, I didn't want to be in a relationship when the show hadn't even aired. Let alone be with someone else from the cast. I was okay with where we were, but I'd be lying if I said I didn't want more.

We continued to spend much time together alone and in group settings. Mostly it was Hope, Caitlin, Kyle, and me. Kyle and I talked about our feelings to other people, and that's how we knew we liked each other. I couldn't get him off my mind.

He even met my little sister. He was good to her, just like he was to me. During Christmas, Divya, Kyle, and I all got COVID and spent the holiday together along with Liney. We spent New Year's Eve together, which led to my birthday. It was not always easy to continue hanging out with him because my feelings for him had continued to grow stronger.

I wanted more time before the show aired and before everything changed. But that February came too quickly. It was all starting to unfold. Season two of *Love Is Blind* finally aired, and Kyle and I watched it together. We would wake up at 3:00 a.m. to binge-watch the show on the day it aired. He barely even watched it while my eyes were glued to the screen. You know when you hear yourself back on a recording, you cringe? Now multiply that by a hundred because that's how cringed I felt. I don't think I'll watch that show ever again.

As I was cringing and judging myself, Kyle would say the sweetest things to me. "You look great," he would say. When I questioned how I could've even picked Shake, he would remind me that I didn't know any better at the time.

At this point, I rarely spoke to Shake. We had one encounter before it aired where he broke down and said, "Deeps, I hope you have my back."

In retrospect, this felt like he knew he fucked up and was trying to get me on his good side; I honestly didn't care. I would make a choice based on what I saw on the screen. I told him I would not blindly do whatever he asked of me. I was fed up with Shake because of how he looked at and talked to women. He had no filter. He would comment on women's bodies without thinking about how it would impact them. He didn't respect women. If he faced any type of rejection, he retaliated. It wasn't always what he said, but it was also how he said it—condescendingly. One time when we were out, he spilled a drink on a girl accidently and proceeded to lick her entire body—from her stomach to the top of her neck to clean it off without even giving her a chance to back away. It was incredibly uncomfortable to witness.

Kyle constantly reminded me not to judge myself, and that was the most comforting thing someone can do for you when the words are hard to say to yourself. There was one scene aired when in my interview, I mentioned I was looking forward to seeing Kyle. He wasn't at the group meetup in Mexico, so he heard this for the first time. I remember he pulled me in for a hug and told me how cute that was. This deepened my attraction to him; still, I couldn't tell him exactly how I felt.

Again, we expressed our feelings to each other through our friends. I'd hear from someone in the group that he couldn't stop thinking about me. That gave me butterflies. But why couldn't he tell me himself? I knew the answer. I always assumed it was the same reason I couldn't. I didn't want to lose him as a friend and complicate the relationship. But his energy electrified me.

When the show aired, Kyle and I gravitated toward each other even more. We traveled together for the first time outside of Chicago to film the *Love Is Blind* reunion. I specifically requested a room next to Kyle in the hotel. Experiencing new things together bonded us. It was the first time

we were both going through something like this. We were
now being aired on Netflix. Our social media was blowing
up. Many people were trying to engage with us and give us
their opinions. These were all strangers, but their words
impacted us. It was new territory. These were foreign roads
to us and having someone by your side to navigate them
with is comforting. It creates a special connection, and
that's what we had. We just wanted to be friends; for now,
there were enough complications in our lives.

I was dealing with Shake and his nonsense at this time.
I watched what Shake had to say about me, along with the
rest of the world. His comment in Mexico, where he said,
"She's like my aunt," was by far the least insulting one. I
knew Shake had said nasty things about me to his castmates when filming, but I wasn't sure what. When he says
that he got a bad edit, he's sadly mistaken. He got a good
one. I later heard from castmates and producers that Shake
compared me to an animal—a flying squirrel—because of
my stretch marks and saggy skin. I heard that he also said
that my body needed to be studied by science. These
comments never made it on air. Nor did many of the other
awful things he said about me.

After that, I avoided interactions with Shake. I deliber-
ately didn't attend the lake house weekend because I
wanted to avoid seeing him. I managed to stay away from
him until a few weeks before the reunion. I didn't want an
enemy out of him; I just knew we couldn't be close. It
doesn't mean that I didn't care. Finding out what he said
about me brought me back to my insecure days, but I didn't
allow myself to stay in that mindset for long. And truth be
told, the support I was getting from my family, friends, and

even fans of the show helped remind me that I wasn't alone. It also reminded me that I wasn't the only one who saw just how horrible Shake could be.

When we started filming *After the Altar*, my feelings for Kyle skyrocketed. Through watching the show and dealing with all the drama, our lives got even more intertwined. We were forced to talk about our feelings. There were so many questions about our relationship. This got my mind racing. I had to address how I felt. I started wondering if there was a future together with this connection. As you've likely picked up by now, I didn't like to express my emotions, and it seemed he didn't either. Our actions spoke louder than words ever would.

I find it interesting that words of affirmation are one of my love languages. I probably need someone to be good at expressing their love in words since I'm so bad at it. Sometimes, I just really wanted to hear from Kyle that he liked me as more than a friend. It felt like we were a couple, so why weren't we? As we continued filming and I was forced to address my feelings, I became determined to talk. We were so intertwined already, so I demanded a decision; otherwise, I wanted to move on. He said he didn't want to lose me. I felt the same way. And that's when our relationship deepened, and we became official.

After filming for *After the Altar* wrapped, we planned to travel together. We both wanted to be out in LA, and with summer around the corner, there were many things to look forward to. We went to our first Coachella festival together.

That was the first time we stayed in the same hotel room together, and our relationship was moving quickly. This added a whole new dynamic.

Oddly, I overanalyzed a lot during this time. The show had just aired. We were getting recognized everywhere we went. The tabloids started picking us up, reporting where we were, and speculating about our relationship status. There was a lot of pressure, and we couldn't even confirm or deny anything about ourselves.

Relationships are even more complicated when you're in the public eye. Everyone has an opinion, and you must keep a stiff upper lip to get through—especially the ugly parts. People seem to think that we don't have real emotions. The keyboard warriors tend not to realize that their hateful words impact our lives. Many men direct messaged me on Instagram, and Kyle probably had the same thing with women. We ended up staying in LA after the festival and enjoyed life and meeting new people. I was still working from home, but I was distracted by the monumental turn in my life.

When we got back to Chicago, it was even more apparent that there was no chance we wouldn't get recognized if we were in public. We were handling it all the best we could. Still, certain insecurities of mine would occasionally flare up again due to all the women approaching him. Kyle is a flirtatious person, and I am an observer, especially concerning body language. We were navigating a new lifestyle and challenged each other to think outside the box. We were setting new goals and reaching new limits. But, with this territory came many temptations. I sometimes felt that Kyle enjoyed being single more than being in a relationship. This was okay with me, but I needed to hear that from him, and I never did.

Kyle and I loved LA when we were out there, so we started planning to return. While apartment hunting for a temporary place, we did some of the most incredible things. I got the opportunity to throw the first pitch on opening weekend for the Chicago Cubs. This was a day that I'll cherish forever. Kyle helped me practice, and I even invited his parents to come watch as we were both on the mound with Danielle and Nick. I had met his parents multiple times beforehand, and it was great to enjoy that moment with them and Divya.

I cared for Kyle greatly; these fantastic opportunities will be some of my most incredible memories. We got to go to Blackhawk, Chicago Fire, and Chicago White Sox games. We got to experience walking out on Soldier Field and see where the Chicago Bears did their sportscasting. We were invited to amazing events and saw incredible performers in concert. We explored new restaurants with our friends. It was an exciting and eventful time in both of our lives, and it was even better that we got to do it together. We rented an apartment in LA for three weeks just to get out of Chicago for a while and walk new paths. While temporarily living in LA, we were free to do whatever we wanted.

I decided to quit my job. I was half-heartedly working and trying to gain insight into what I wanted for my future. I loved my job as a data analyst but was ready to embark on a new career path. I could always come back to technology. I could incorporate what I learned in this field and use it in my future career moves.

This is why I quit my job and opened my LLC. I was

ready to start showing up for myself. I was given a platform to make a difference and wanted to explore how I could use it to do some good. While figuring it out, we put our energy into hobbies.

Kyle and I loved photography. He was much better at it than me, which was part of the fun. I loved his ability to teach me new things and see life through a different aperture. We walked everywhere, which was the perfect time for honest conversations. Even the silence was peaceful. We would get recognized in most public places. We didn't mind because people were genuine and kind toward us.

We were soon spending all our time together, which wasn't healthy. Alone time recharges me and allows me to come back to myself. And we both weren't getting that. We sensed the energy was off. Sometimes I felt him withdrawing, which increased my anxiety, triggering my old abandonment issues. I thought I had dealt with this aspect that seemed to haunt my dreams of being in a healthy relationship.

Looking back, I think I needed to hear Kyle's feelings, those words of reassurance. Perhaps it wasn't enough for him to just show me through his acts of service. This, paired with Kyle's flirtatious nature, severely impacted me and our relationship. It gave me mixed signals—on the one hand, I know he loved being around me, but on the other, I could see he loved the attention he got from others. It left me confused and in an insecure state of mind.

We had experienced beautiful moments of joy, intimacy, and adventures together, but very quickly, things started to change between us. This was when I realized that although we had been spending lots of time together, we weren't really talking about the important stuff that helps make a relationship last. We didn't communicate our wants, love languages, or habits that made us happy. We both needed to vocalize what we wanted, and, in my view, Kyle wanted to be single to explore other options and figure out what he wanted. I wanted to be in a relationship with someone who had the same mindset, goals, and aspirations as I did. We were on completely different pages.

It was easier to end things and remain friends than try to mend this mess. And one day, we had a conversation and agreed that just going back to being friends would be easier for both of us. A heavy weight lifted off my shoulders during that talk. I could finally stop pretending everything was okay. Kyle bought a one-way ticket back to Chicago later that day, and I remained back in LA, processing everything that had transpired. The next day I returned to Chicago, not realizing everything would now change.

While I knew breaking up was the right decision, I still had many days where I missed Kyle. There were nights I just lay awake wishing he was next to me, realizing that may never happen again. Even though I knew I should be happy we had those sweet memories together, nostalgia crept in, making it hard to suppress thoughts of him. I know we both learned lessons from each other to become better versions of ourselves. And there was much more to learn from this life. We recognized that for this to happen, we couldn't do it together. We had to take different paths.

Not too long after we ended our relationship, I was getting messages and pictures of him with other women. It's hard to see the person you care about move on so quickly and in a public way. It was clear that going back to the friendship we once had was too difficult. Feelings don't just turn off like a light switch, and I needed time to myself without him.

I could see he was putting in a different kind of romantic effort, unlike with me. Kyle was taking women on thoughtful dates, buying flowers, and spending money. He never did these things with or for me. Seeing him take other women to the same places we had visited, do the same activities we loved, meet his parents, and go to the same studios with the same photographers was too painful to witness. It was certainly not healthy for me.

Sometimes, it's simply too hard to stay friends when lingering feelings exist. I was trying to move on, as well. I went on dates and started seeing someone else. I was trying my best to distract myself from my deep feelings for him. I realized that I must look inward to heal, not to others.

Maybe one day, Kyle and I will find our way back to each other and become the main characters of the same book. Or perhaps we will read two different novels about each other from afar. I know that letting go will take me one step closer to figuring out if we'll return to each other, even as friends. Kyle knows he was the exact chapter I needed in my life. I'm grateful for what we shared. And now it's finally time to write the next page with new characters.

AFTER ALL THAT

"In three words I can sum up everything
I've learned about life, it goes on."
– ROBERT FROST

What a wild ride these past two years have been.

Honestly, what a wild ride these thirty-one years of life have been!

I found myself packing up my things to leave the country I was born in. It turned out to be a pivotal decision for my family.

I found myself landing in a foreign place called America. It turned out to be a country that shaped so much of who I am today.

I found myself in a pod, falling in love with a stranger. It turned out that he wasn't the one I was supposed to marry.

I now find myself ... well, the story continues, and I

don't know the ending. I don't know the next chapter, for that matter.

I do find myself reconnecting with my younger self more these days. I remember being that carefree little girl many years ago in India. My thoughts didn't impact my actions. I was happy just being myself, doing the things I loved, like playing in the mud, riding a bike, or helping my mom cook. I took pleasure in being in the moment and enjoying myself because I wasn't old enough to understand what it meant to think about the future.

I know that in this next stage of life, I want to bring back the mindset of that little girl. I want to continue to explore my roots and embrace the culture I once ran from. I want to continue working harder to be the most authentic version of myself.

Sometimes, I wish I could go back and tell my teenage self that everything will work out just fine and not to worry. I want to tell her to stop trying to grow up too fast, to embrace who she is, and not let outside voices dictate who she chooses to be. Most of all, I wish I could hug her.

Three decades of life have been quite the journey, and I know I'm just getting started in many ways. I've made my fair share of mistakes along the way, but each experience has helped me connect more deeply to who I am as a person and what matters most to me. I had to go through the lows to learn to appreciate the highs. I had to experience heartbreak to understand what true love was and, more importantly, what it wasn't. I had to experience the act of rebelling against my family to learn in the end, that family has and always will be the most important part of my life. I had to experience insincere friendships to know how to recognize the meaningful ones.

I realize that I can't control what others may think of me. All I can do is show up as my best self in each moment and continue to learn and be better. And ultimately, I recognize that if I don't treat myself with love and compassion, how can I expect anyone else to?

And while at some points along my journey, I've asked, *Why is this happening to me?* I realize now that all these things weren't happening to me, they were happening *for* me. If my story had looked any differently, I wouldn't be taking the stage to do a TED talk, I wouldn't be releasing a podcast, and I certainly wouldn't be writing this book. Because of all my experiences, I'm now determined to use my platform to help encourage others to rise above their circumstances and choose to love themselves no matter what.

Every day we wake up, we have a choice. Will we dare to dream big and celebrate who we are? Or will we shy away and hide our potential? Will we choose to let someone else's opinion of us define us? Or will we choose to define ourselves?

I've made my choice. Today and always, *I choose myself.* My hope in sharing my story is that you choose to do the same.

ACKNOWLEDGMENTS

Through this incredible journey of life, I see that every single person that I have met has made a beautiful impact in shaping the woman I am today.

My Amma (Mom), Gayatri Vempati, you are the best mother anyone could have. I know everyone says that, and they are entitled to it. No one loves you as a mother does, and you have proven that to me every single moment of my life. The way you care for others and the grace you show while doing it is why I am who I am today. You always saw the good in me, even through my mischief, rebellion, and attitudes. You always knew my potential and your tender and tough love demonstrated that your care for me far exceeds anyone else's I'll ever have in this lifetime. I am so grateful for your continued support and love. I still have so much to learn from you.

My Nana (Dad), Venkat Vempati, your kind-hearted spirit, and your playful nature are why I have the personality I do. Your dad jokes, laughter, dancing, and curiosity to learn and provide have certainly improved my life. I am grateful for your unconditional love, hard work ethic, and ability to light up a room.

I also wish to thank my brother Sunny and his beautiful wife, Hina, for putting up with me through my adventures. The way you both tackle life and exemplify what it means to constantly set new goals and go after them is something I truly admire. You are like a second set of parents to me and the best friends I know I'll have forever in my life. The gift of this bond is extraordinary, and I hope you know how much I truly cherish you. You showed me love and support, which I will never forget. I am so proud to have people like you in my life.

And my little sister, Divya. Life would not be the same without you. You are not just my sister; you are my therapist, my rock, my best friend, and my soulmate. I am so proud of the woman you are and continue to become. I learn from you every day, and I hope you know the support you give me is irreplaceable. There are countless nights where you have been my emotional support through my anxiety. The hours you spent with me writing this book and the unconditional love you gave me are things I will never take for granted.

The wisest decision I made was to listen to my best friend, Derek, who sent me a posting for a dating show. My life has changed dramatically because of this small but magnanimous decision. Thank you, Derek.

To my friends, both the old and new, I hope you know the memories we shared so far have seeped permanently into my soul. The family I choose is you. There is still a lifetime of experiences to go, and I am lucky to share those congruent paths with each and every one of you. Along the way, I know that all of you will be my guiding light through all the tough times, as you've been before. In return, I will continuously be of support to you.

A huge thank you goes to Katie Zeppieri Beckett, my publicist, and publisher at The MicDrop Agency. She spent many hours reading and editing this book, publishing it, and helping me speak about my experiences. Thank you from the bottom of my heart.

Thanks to my detail-oriented editor, Patricia Ogilvie of Prorisk Enterprises Ltd., for crossing my t's and dotting my i's. You make my story sound smooth, and for this, I appreciate you.

Lastly, I want to thank my followers and everyone who has reached out to me with love and support. Your kind words have inspired me to continue sharing my life in a public way. The moving messages I've received from so many of you have permanently made a mark on my heart. Your stories motivate me to be a better person and be vulnerable enough to share my mistakes and accomplishments. I truly feel the loving energy from so many of you out there. I hope you know how much I appreciate every single person who has reached out to me. I've spent countless hours reading your messages and crying, knowing that there are people out there, just like me, who are going through hardships and persevering despite them. Our shared journeys of courage unite us all, and there is strength and power in that.

Thank you to my cast mates of *Love Is Blind*, the producers, and behind the scenes team of the show, who graciously stood by my side.

There are many more people I wish to acknowledge, but for now, I want to just take a moment to thank all those who have been a lesson in loving myself and seeing my worth.

Any memoir reflects the family and personal relationships that define one's life. And this book was shaped by my family and friends. For without your love and support, I would not be here to write this incredible story. Thank you all.

Finally, I am responsible for the opinions and interpretations expressed in this autobiography. These pages reflect how I experienced the events I described from childhood to now.

Know, too, that my story is just beginning, and I'm excited about it. And until then, I am deeply grateful for having this opportunity to share my story with you.

ABOUT THE AUTHOR

Deepti Vempati is a TEDx speaker, entrepreneur, data analyst, social influencer, and reality TV star best known for her leading role in season two of the hit Netflix show *Love Is Blind*. Fans from across the globe fell in love with Deepti for her authenticity, confidence, and vulnerability. Her powerful words "I'm choosing myself" have become an empowerment motto for thousands of women. With over one million followers on social media (@lifewithdeeps), Deepti uses her platform to inspire others to find their voice and stand up for what they believe in. This is Deepti's first book.

instagram.com/lifewithdeeps

Made in the USA
Monee, IL
17 January 2023

25361973R00111